Know It, Show It

GRADE 4

Printed in the U.S.A.

ISBN 978-1-328-45325-9

12 13 14 15   2591   27 26 25 24 23 22

4500863973   A B C D E F G

Grade
4

Contents

Name _____

Short a and Long a

▶ Read each sentence. Find the word that includes the short or long *a* vowel sound. Underline the vowel or vowel team that makes the sound. After the sentence, underline "Short *a* Sound" or "Long *a* Sound."

1. Did Josh sprain his knee running?

        Short *a* Sound   Long *a* Sound

2. If I make an error in spelling, I just erase it.

        Short *a* Sound   Long *a* Sound

3. This bread is stale.

        Short *a* Sound   Long *a* Sound

4. Mr. Green will remain with the children.

        Short *a* Sound   Long *a* Sound

5. He used a firm grasp to open the jar.

        Short *a* Sound   Long *a* Sound

6. I was amazed that I could climb the rope.

        Short *a* Sound   Long *a* Sound

7. Mom took a break from grilling dinner.

        Short *a* Sound   Long *a* Sound

8. Josie cleaned the drain with vinegar.

        Short *a* Sound   Long *a* Sound

9. We built a strong raft from the wood.

        Short *a* Sound   Long *a* Sound

Critical Vocabulary

▶ **Use your understanding of the Critical Vocabulary words to support your answers to the questions below.**

1. How would you feel if someone treated you with **disdain**?

_____

_____

2. What might you do **inadvertently** while listening to a **mundane** person speak?

_____

_____

3. What are some things that cannot be **consumed**?

_____

_____

4. Tell about a time you **considered** something before you **obliged** to do it.

_____

_____

5. Tell about a time you acted in **defiance**.

_____

_____

6. What are ways you may have **descended** from the second floor to the first floor?

_____

_____

Name _____

7. What is something **profound** you could say to someone you care about?

_____

_____

8. If you were planning a party outside, what might a **cynic** expect to happen?

_____

_____

> **Choose two of the Critical Vocabulary words and use them in a sentence.**

_____

_____

_____

_____

_____

Name _____

Author's Purpose

Knowing the **author's purpose** can help you understand the author's message and main idea.

> **Answer the questions about page 23 in *Flora and Ulysses: The Illuminated Adventures*.**

1. What is the author's purpose for writing *Flora and Ulysses*?

_____

_____

2. What parts of the text support your answer?

_____

_____

> **Answer the questions about page 40 in *Flora and Ulysses: The Illuminated Adventures*.**

3. What message does the author want to share?

_____

_____

4. How do the characters and story events help you understand the message?

_____

_____

_____

Words with Short and Long a

> Use the words from the box to complete the spelling patterns chart for short and long *a*.

quake	class	past	delay
amaze	gray	grasp	break
steak	apple	fail	
plate	grape	crayon	

Short *a* Vowel Sound	Long *a* Vowel Sound/ Open Syllable	Long Vowel/ Consonant/Silent Vowel	Two Vowel Team/ Long Vowel Sound
closed (*last*)	open (*maybe*)	VCe (*blade*)	vowel team (*stain*)

> Pick one word from each column and use it in a sentence. Write the sentences on the lines below.

1. _____

2. _____

3. _____

4. _____

Prefixes un-, in-, im-, re-

> Complete the chart with words that contain the prefixes *un–*, *in–*, *im–*, *re–*.

un–	in–	im–	re–

> Write a sentence for each word in the chart.

_____

_____

_____

_____

_____

_____

_____

_____

_____

_____

Name _____

Text and Graphic Features

Text and graphic features, such as the style and the size of print, can help tell a story or make information clear. Some texts include special type that looks different from the other words on the page. Using special type draws attention to a particular idea, event, or situation.

> Use pages 22–23 in *Flora and Ulysses: The Illuminated Adventures* to answer the questions below.

1. What do you learn through the words and images on pages 22–23?

_____

_____

_____

2. Why might the author have used a graphic novel format to begin the story?

_____

_____

_____

> Revisit page 30 and answer the questions below.

3. What words on page 30 appear in special type?

_____

_____

4. Why did the author use special type for these words?

_____

_____

Name _____

Figurative Language

Authors use **figurative language** to create a special effect or feeling, or they use figurative language to make a point. Figurative language includes figures of speech that compare, exaggerate, or mean something different from what is expected.

> ▶ Read the last two sentences on page 26 in *Flora and Ulysses: The Illuminated Adventures*.

1. How do the words *poof* and *fwump* add to the story?

_____

_____

_____

_____

> ▶ Reread paragraph 41 on page 28.

2. Which part of paragraph 41 shows exaggeration through use of a hyperbole?

_____

_____

_____

_____

3. How does exaggeration help to describe the squirrel's personality?

_____

_____

_____

_____

Short e and Long e

▶ Place the long *e* words in the first column and the short *e* words in the second column.

engine	complete	speck
freedom	west	greed
beast	gleam	speed
fresh	kept	shelf
cheap	member	belief

Long *e*	Short *e*

▶ Write two sentences using the words from the list. Circle the long *e* words and underline the short *e* words in your sentences.

_____

_____

_____

_____

Name _____

Critical Vocabulary

▶ Use your understanding of the Critical Vocabulary words to create a word web for each word. In the center is one of these words. In the outer ovals, write words and phrases that relate to that word. Discuss your word webs with a partner.

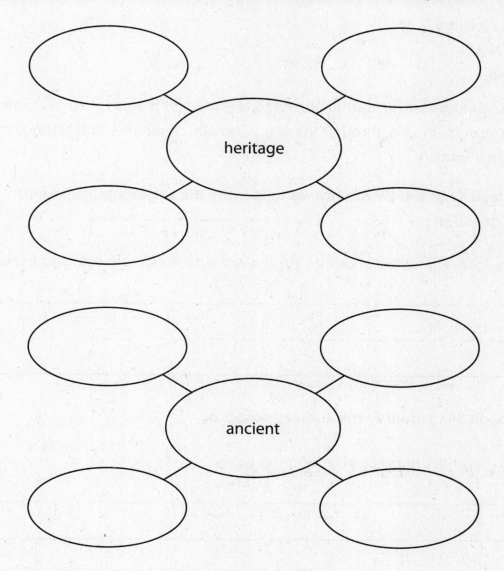

▶ Use the Critical Vocabulary words in sentences of your own.

_____

_____

Name _____

Author's Purpose

An **author's purpose** is the reason why he or she is writing a text. A text can have one or more of these purposes:

- to inform
- to express feelings
- to entertain
- to persuade

Besides having a purpose, an author also has a message for readers. Authors share their message, or main idea, through the words, details, characters, and settings they choose for their writing.

> Reread page 47 in *Yes! We Are Latinos* to identify the authors' purpose and answer the question.

1. How does José Miguel feel about his experience with Roger? How do you know?

_____

_____

_____

> Reread page 54 to identify the authors' purpose.

2. What is the authors' purpose in writing this poem?

_____

_____

_____

3. What message do the authors want to share with readers?

_____

_____

Name **Victoria**

Point of View

It's important to know from whose **point of view** the events are told. That's because different people can tell the same story different ways!

Stories are often told from a first-person or a third-person point of view.

First-Person Point of View The narrator . . .	Third-Person Point of View The narrator . . .
is a character in the story.	is someone outside the story.
tells his or her own thoughts and feelings.	tells the thoughts and feelings of others.
uses pronouns such as *I, me, my, mine,* and *we*.	uses pronouns such as *he, she,* and *they*.

▷ **Reread page ~~60~~ 52 in *The Year of the Rat* to answer the questions.**

1. Who is the narrator in this part of the story? From what point of view is this part of the story told? Give examples to support your answer.

Grace lin is someone Outside the story. The Part of story is Being told in third Person. I Know this Because Pronouns ~~the her~~ 55

▷ **Reread page 63 and think about how the point of view changes.**

2. Who is the narrator in this part of the story? From what point of view is this part of the story told? Why do you think the author tells the story from this point of view now?

The narrator is pacy. This Part of story is told in fist person. this author tells the story her own thought. 37

▷ **Reread page 65 to practice determining point of view in a text.**

3. What is the point of view in "Knowing the Fish"? How do you know?

_____

Name _____

Prefixes *mis-*, *pre-*, *dis-*

> Complete the chart with words that contain the prefixes *mis–*, *pre–*, *dis–*.

mis–	pre–	dis–

> Write a sentence for each word in the chart.

_____

_____

_____

_____

_____

_____

_____

_____

_____

_____

_____

_____

Name _____

Character

Characters are the people or animals in a story. As characters deal with a conflict, readers see how one event causes another event to happen and how characters find a resolution.

> **Reread page 64 in *The Year of the Rat* and identify Pacy's conflict.**

1. What is Pacy's conflict at this point of the story? How does Dad try to help her?

_____

_____

_____

> **Reread page 68 to answer the following questions about Pacy's character.**

2. What reason does Pacy give for wanting to work alone? What does her reason show about her?

_____

_____

3. What do you learn about Pacy when she says she will be an author and illustrator "no matter what"?

_____

_____

> **Reread page 71 to look for details about how Pacy's character changes.**

4. How do Pacy's thoughts about Becky and Charlotte show that she has changed?

_____

_____

_____

Name _____

Short *i* and Long *i*

> Sort the Spelling Words correctly. Which words have a short *i* sound, and which words have a long *i* sound?

Short *i*	Long *i*

> Complete the sentence by choosing the correct word. Write the correct word on the line.

1. A new lamp will _____ the room.

2. A strong _____ blew for hours.

3. The book club must _____ which book to read.

4. The low temperatures caused a _____ in the air.

5. There was a wide _____ on the side of the road.

6. Our town decided to _____ a new skating rink.

7. Long ago a _____ wheel was used to turn thread into cloth.

8. Beautiful handwriting requires _____.

Spelling Words

witness
skill
decide
ticket
live
brighten
spinning
sigh
ditch
build
chill
remind
inch
surprise
wind

Literary Elements

All stories have a certain structure. **Literary elements** such as character, plot, and setting form this structure. Elements of structure vary from story to story, though. For example, the culture in which a story is set can influence the story's plot. Also, interactions among characters and the changes they undergo influence a story.

> **Reread page 80 in *Kitoto the Mighty* and answer the question about the story structure.**

1. How has the author crafted the story structure?

_____

_____

> **Reread paragraphs 17–19 and look at the illustrations. Then answer the question about story details.**

2. What details help describe the cultural setting of the folktale?

_____

_____

> **Reread page 87 and answer the question about Kitoto's character.**

3. How does Kitoto's character change again when faced with the "giant"? What is the reason for this change?

_____

_____

> **Reread page 88 and answer the question about the story structure.**

4. How would you describe the story structure of this folktale?

_____

Name _____

Suffixes –y and –ly

▷ Complete the chart with words that contain the suffixes –y, –ly.

–y	–ly

▷ Write a sentence for each word in the chart.

_____

_____

_____

_____

_____

_____

_____

Name _____

Critical Vocabulary

You can use the words you learn from reading as you talk and write.

> Use details from *The Science Behind Sight* to support your answers to the questions below. Then use the Critical Vocabulary words as you talk with a partner about your answers.

1. What would happen if light did not **reflect** off solid objects?

_____

2. Which would you describe as **transparent**, a brick wall or a window? Explain.

_____

3. Why is it easier to **judge** the distance between two objects with both eyes at the front of your head?

_____

_____

4. What would you use to **illuminate** a large area?

_____

5. Would you need a **luminous** object to read a book if you were in a bright room? Why or why not?

_____

_____

> Choose two of the Critical Vocabulary words and use them in a sentence.

_____

_____

Name _____

Text and Graphic Features

Informational text often includes **text features** such as headings and boldfaced words. Informational text usually includes one or more **graphic features** such as photographs, diagrams, and illustrations.

> **Answer the questions about page 115 of *The Science Behind Sight*.**

1. How does the diagram connect to the text in the caption?

_____

_____

2. How does the diagram add to your understanding of the ideas in paragraph 16?

_____

_____

> **Choose another diagram in *The Science Behind Sight*.**

3. What does the diagram explain?

_____

_____

4. How does the diagram add to your understanding of the text?

_____

_____

Short and Long o Sounds

> Read each sentence. Under the blank are the words "Short o Sound" or "Long o Sound." Find a word from the box that contains that vowel sound and makes sense in the sentence. Write the word in the blank.

Short o Sound	Long o Sound
frosty	bowling
lobby	grove
plodded	protested
softened	toasted

1. The school's _____ area is by the front door.
   Short o Sound

2. The sound in the _____ alley was like thunder.
   Long o Sound

3. I _____ toward the car, dragging my feet all the way.
   Short o Sound

4. This _____ of trees is home to lots of wildlife.
   Long o Sound

5. Mark _____ some bread for breakfast.
   Long o Sound

6. The _____ winter air felt clean and crisp.
   Short o Sound

7. Sara whined and _____ her early bedtime.
   Long o Sound

8. The butter _____ and melted under the hot sun.
   Short o Sound

Name _____

Latin Root *lumin*

The words *luminous* and *illuminates* contain a root that has Latin origins.
The meaning of the root *lumin* is "light."

> ▶ **Complete the chart with other words that contain the root *lumin*.**

lumin
_____
_____
_____
_____

> ▶ **Write a sentence for each word in the chart.**

_____

_____

_____

_____

_____

_____

_____

_____

_____

_____

Name _____

Syllable Division Patterns: VCCV, VCV, VV

> Read each sentence. Look carefully at the underlined word. Write the underlined word in the correct column to show which syllable division pattern it follows.

Sentence	VCCV	VCV	VV
1. There was an old trunk in the <u>attic</u>.			
2. Each year our class has a <u>poetry</u> festival.			
3. The <u>lion</u> is native to Africa.			
4. I try <u>never</u> to be late for school.			
5. A farmer uses a <u>tractor</u> to plow his fields.			
6. Our dog is a <u>rescue</u> from the shelter.			
7. The <u>dentist</u> told us to brush our teeth more often.			
8. The kitten's fur was as smooth as <u>velvet</u>.			
9. There is a <u>hotel</u> near the airport.			
10. She was in a hurry to <u>open</u> the package.			

Critical Vocabulary

You can use the words you learn from reading as you talk and write.

▶ **Use your understanding of the Critical Vocabulary words to support your answers to the questions below. Then use the Critical Vocabulary words as you talk with a partner about your answers.**

1. What is something you **relish**?

_____

_____

2. What **familiar** object can't you do without?

_____

_____

3. What time of year do you **savor** most?

_____

_____

4. How might you **enhance** your chances of doing well on a test?

_____

_____

▶ **Write a sentence using two Critical Vocabulary words below.**

_____

_____

Name _____

Media Techniques

Media is the means of communication through radio, newspapers, television, magazines, and the Internet. **Media techniques** are the methods through which information is communicated. Media techniques include sound and visual elements, live action, animation, and information.

▶ **Answer the following questions about** *Animal Senses*.

1. How does the video help you understand more about the animal sense of hearing?

_____

_____

_____

_____

2. How does the video help you understand more about the animal sense of touch?

_____

_____

_____

_____

_____

3. How is the video helpful in understanding more about animal sounds?

_____

_____

_____

_____

Name _____

Words with Syllable Division Patterns: VCCV, VCV, VV

> **Choose the word with the given syllable division pattern to complete the sentence. Write the word on the line.**

1. The riverbank was _____ and steep.   VCCV
muddy   wet

2. The farmer's field was full of _____.   VCV
wheat   clover

3. A carpenter uses a _____ in his work.   VCCV
saw   hammer

4. The _____ took a nap in the warm sun.   VV
tiger   lion

5. We could smell the _____ cooking in the kitchen.   VCV
bacon   waffles

6. Our music teacher will play the _____ for our class concert.   VV
piano   trumpet

7. In science class, we used _____ for our experiment.   VCCV
magnets   heat

8. She has a great _____ for high-speed transportation.   VV
plan   idea

Words with Vowels Sounds /ŭ/, /yo͞o/, and /o͞o/

> Circle the word or words with the short *u* sound in each sentence.

1. What a beautiful bunch of grapes!

2. The mule got stuck in the ditch.

3. A trunk is useful to an elephant.

4. I trust people who tell the truth.

5. Scatter the crumbs for the ducks.

6. The man in the truck was hungry.

7. It is fun to amuse the baby.

8. We played with the puppies for hours.

9. If we are lucky, we'll be home for lunch.

10. Aunt Ruth told me to brush my hair.

Name _____ Victoria

Critical Vocabulary

You can use the words you learn from reading as you talk and write.

> **Use your understanding of the Critical Vocabulary words to support your answers to the questions below. Then use the Critical Vocabulary words as you talk with a partner about your answers.**

1. What's the difference between a silly situation and an **absurd** situation?

_____

_____

2. What would you do if you witnessed one classmate **taunt** another?

_____

3. Why might someone **forfeit** the chance to win a new bike?

_____

_____

4. What foods have you **despised** in the past but now enjoy eating?

_____

5. What would you do if you think an approaching dog might be **ferocious**?

_____

6. When have you prepared **elaborately** for an event?

_____

7. What would you want if you could have anything you **coveted**?

_____

> **Write a sentence using two Critical Vocabulary words below.**

_____

Name _Victoria (3) 21Oct 2023 mon_

Plot

Most stories include the same main parts, or elements. Story elements include **plot**, the series of events that make up the story. In a plot, the **rising action** builds as readers learn the story's problem. The action reaches a **climax** when the tension in the story is the greatest. In the story's **falling action**, readers learn about the **resolution**, or how the story's problem is solved.

In historical fiction, characters are from another time and place, or **setting**. The characters give readers insight as to how people of that time might have thought, spoken, and acted. Often, events that happen at the time of the story's setting have a great impact on characters' lives.

> **Read page 144 in *The Game of Silence* and answer the following question.**

1. What details tell you about the historical setting? How does the setting add to the story's plot?

   The game of silence takes Place in the year 1800 on lake such The story follows the ojibwe trich and how they react to being

> **Read paragraphs 8–11 in *The Game of Silence* and answer the following questions.**

2. What details show how Omakayas and Pinch get along? _read 116-111 and_

   Omakayas and pinch get along being by playing game of silence. Push off their land

3. Why are these details part of the rising action?

   The rising action is when the visitors arrived

4. Which events tell the falling action?

   The falling action is when the grandmother said you can quit after we eat because this falling action

Name _____

Suffixes –y and –ly

> Complete the chart with words that contain the suffix –y or –ly.

–y	–ly

> Write a sentence for each word in the chart.

_____

_____

_____

_____

_____

_____

_____

Name _____

Figurative Language

Figurative language is the use of words and phrases beyond their everyday meaning. The chart shows some examples.

	What It Is	Example
Simile	Uses the words *like* or *as* to compare two things	In the freezing air, my breath looked like puffy white clouds.
Metaphor	Compares two things or ideas, without using *like* or *as*	The still, quiet lake was a mirror.
Imagery	Uses words that appeal to the sense of sight, hearing, smell, taste, and touch	She smiled as the rich, sweet scent of cinnamon and apples filled the air.

Authors use figurative language to help readers imagine or understand ideas in a new or different way. Figurative language also helps readers notice an author's voice, or way of using language.

> **Reread paragraph 4 in *The Game of Silence* and answer the following questions.**

1. What words and phrases does the author use that appeal to the senses?

_____

_____

2. What does this sensory language help you understand?

_____

_____

3. Identify a metaphor in this paragraph and explain its meaning.

_____

_____

Words with Vowels Sounds /ŭ/, /yо̅о̅/, and /о̅о̅/

> Read each sentence. Find a word from the box that makes sense in the sentence. Write the word in the blank. Then circle the sound the word makes: /ŭ/, /yо̅о̅/, or /о̅о̅/.

bunch	juice	stew	rescue	under
refuse	trust	argue	rude	dew
brush	clue	truth	tune	trunk

1. When you say you will not do something, you _____ .
   /ŭ/ /yо̅о̅/ /о̅о̅/

2. Another name for a melody is a _____ .
   /ŭ/ /yо̅о̅/ /о̅о̅/

3. Another word for a group is a _____ .
   /ŭ/ /yо̅о̅/ /о̅о̅/

4. The liquid squeezed from ripe fruit is called _____ .
   /ŭ/ /yо̅о̅/ /о̅о̅/

5. To save someone from danger is to _____ them.
   /ŭ/ /yо̅о̅/ /о̅о̅/

6. Aunt Terry keeps a spare tire in the _____ of her car.
   /ŭ/ /yо̅о̅/ /о̅о̅/

7. I looked for a _____ in the story to find out what the
   /ŭ/ /yо̅о̅/ /о̅о̅/
   word meant.

8. Mom knows she can _____ me to feed the dog every morning.
   /ŭ/ /yо̅о̅/ /о̅о̅/

Name _____

Author's Craft

Author's craft is the language and techniques a writer uses to make his or her writing interesting and communicate ideas to the reader. Sometimes authors use **literal language** to express ideas in a text. There are other techniques that are used as part of an author's craft. The table below shows different techniques used by authors as they write.

Technique	Definition
Voice	The author's style that makes his or her writing unique
Mood	The emotions and feelings the author wants the reader to have while reading the text
Anecdote	A short, funny, or interesting story related to what's currently happening or being discussed
Language	Vocabulary, precise nouns, sensory words, and vivid verbs that make the text more interesting
Hyperbole	Exaggerations that make things sound bigger, better, or more than what they truly are

> **Reread page 152 and answer the following questions.**

1. What phrases and other literal language does the author use to describe the gathering in paragraph 14?

_____

_____

_____

2. What purpose does this literal language and imagery serve?

_____

_____

_____

_____

Name _____

Vowel Sounds o͝o and o͞o

> Read each sentence. Find the word that includes the sound of o͝o or o͞o. Underline the letter or group of letters that stand for that sound. Below the sentence, underline the kind of sound you hear in the word.

1. My favorite kind of food is pizza.

   o͝o   o͞o

2. Does your dad prefer butter or sauce on his noodles?

   o͝o   o͞o

3. Louis is a very talented violin player.

   o͝o   o͞o

4. What a delicious cookie!

   o͝o   o͞o

5. Connor is in a bad mood when he doesn't get enough sleep.

   o͝o   o͞o

6. When Amad went fishing, he put a worm on his hook.

   o͝o   o͞o

7. What kind of books does Sara like to read?

   o͝o   o͞o

8. My bedroom is painted in a lovely purple.

   o͝o   o͞o

9. Erica needs to look in both directions before she crosses the street.

   o͝o   o͞o

10. Hannah knows that she should always try her best.

    o͝o   o͞o

Multiple Syllable Words with Vowel Sounds o͝o, o͞o

▶ Read each sentence. At the end of each sentence is the vowel sound o͝o or o͞o. Find a word from the box that contains this vowel sound and makes sense in the sentence. Write that word in the blank.

o͝o	o͞o
woodwork	caboose
graceful	poodle
octopus	youthful
scrapbook	amuse
pudding	tulips

1. Jessica is excited for spring, when the _____ in her garden will bloom. (o͞o)

2. The _____ dancer seemed to float across the stage. (o͞o)

3. Do you like chocolate _____ ? (o͝o)

4. The train had a red _____ . (o͞o)

5. Many animals live in the ocean, including the whale and the _____ . (o͝o)

6. My friend's dog is a black _____ . (o͞o)

7. I enjoy reading funny books because they _____ me. (o͞o)

8. The _____ was filled with pictures from my mom's childhood. (o͝o)

Suffixes –ful, –ous, –less

▶ Complete the chart with other words that contain each suffix.

–ful	_–ous_	_–less_
successful	adventurous	lifeless

▶ Write a short story with words using the three suffixes.

_____

_____

_____

_____

_____

_____

Name _____Victoria 18,OCT2023 Wed_____

Point of View

Point of view is the way authors tell about events. In firsthand accounts, authors tell about events that they have seen in person. Authors tell these accounts using first-person pronouns such as *I*, *me*, and *my*. In secondhand accounts, authors were not present at the events. Instead they tell what happened to other people and what they said about it. Authors use third-person pronouns such as *he, she, him, her, they,* and *them.*

▶ **Reread paragraphs 5 and 6 of** *The Galveston Hurricane of 1900.*

Pg.128

1. Which part of this text is a firsthand account? How do you know?

Paragraph 6 is a firsthand accoutt the author theuses the pronouns we and us.

2. Which part is a secondhand account? How do you know?

The author. How I know this because the author is talking about information.

▶ **Compare the information given in the firsthand account to the information given in the secondhand account.**

3. What details do you learn in the firsthand account that are not included in the secondhand account?

Firsthand account

▶ **Reread paragraph 15 of** *The Galveston Hurricane of 1900.*

4. Is paragraph 15 a firsthand account or a secondhand account? How do you know?

Secondhand account. I know this because the author wasn't their at that time.

Name _____

Two-Syllable Words with the Vowel Sounds /ou/ and /ô/

> Read each sentence. Find the word that includes the sound of /ou/ or /ô/. Underline the letter or group of letters that stands for the sound. Below the sentence, underline the kind of sound you hear in the word you underlined.

1. My dad used the chainsaw to trim the large tree.
   /ou/   /ô/

2. Do you prefer walking or riding in a car?
   /ou/   /ô/

3. The banker put the money into the savings account.
   /ou/   /ô/

4. "I feel lousy!" said Marcus.
   /ou/   /ô/

5. My grandmother makes a delicious clam chowder.
   /ou/   /ô/

6. I made a sandwich because I was hungry.
   /ou/   /ô/

7. I am doubtful that I will be able to attend.
   /ou/   /ô/

8. The princess lived in the highest tower.
   /ou/   /ô/

9. The medicine tasted awful!
   /ou/   /ô/

10. Talking is not permitted in the library.
    /ou/   /ô/

Critical Vocabulary

You can use the words you learn from reading as you talk and write.

> **Use your understanding of the Critical Vocabulary words to support your answers to the questions below.**

1. How do people behave **adoringly** toward others?

   _____

   _____

2. In what ways does a person need to be **capable** in order to drive a car?

   _____

   _____

3. Have you ever been a **spectator** at a big event? Did you enjoy it? Why or why not?

   _____

   _____

4. What do you regard with **disbelief**? Why?

   _____

   _____

> **Choose two of the Critical Vocabulary words and use them in sentences. Include a synonym and/or an antonym for each vocabulary word you use.**

   _____

   _____

Name _____

Elements of Drama

A play, sometimes known as a **drama**, is a story that is written to be performed by actors in front of an audience. Dramas have elements that help people perform the story. A **cast of characters** lists each character in the play. The name of each character appears before the words he or she says. These words are called **dialogue**. **Stage settings** tell the audience where and when each scene takes place. **Stage directions** tell the actors what to do and how to speak.

▶ **Reread page 207 in *Catch Me If You Can*. Then answer the question.**

1. How do the words and their arrangement on the page look different from other stories or poems?

_____
_____
_____
_____
_____

▶ **Reread page 209 in *Catch Me If You Can*. Then answer the questions.**

2. What event is taking place in this part of the play?

_____

3. Which characters are speaking?

_____

4. What do the stage directions tell the spectators to do?

_____
_____

Name _____

Latin Roots vis, aud, spec

> Complete the chart with other words that contain each root.

vis	aud	spec
vision	audio	spectrum

> Write sentences with words using the three roots.

_____

_____

_____

_____

_____

Name _____

Idioms, Adages, and Proverbs

Idioms, adages, and proverbs are types of common sayings that have meanings beyond what can be understood by their individual words. An **idiom** means something different from what the words say. An **adage** expresses a truth or gives advice. A **proverb** expresses a short truth based on common sense or experience.

> **Reread page 206 in *Catch Me If You Can*. Then answer the questions.**

1. What adage can you identify? What does this saying mean?

_____

_____

2. What does this saying mean in relation to the text?

_____

_____

> **Reread page 208 in *Catch Me If You Can*. Then answer the questions.**

3. What proverb or idiom appears in the dialogue of Young John?

_____

4. What does Young John mean?

_____

5. What proverb or idiom does Atalanta say? What does Atalanta mean?

_____

6. How would the meaning of each expression be different if you thought about the meaning of each individual word?

_____

_____

Name _____

Literary Elements

Literary elements include characters in a story, the setting, the plot, and the events that happen in the story.

> Reread paragraphs 14 and 15 of *My Diary from Here to There*. Then answer the question.

1. How do the events add to the story's plot?

_____

_____

_____

_____

_____

_____

_____

> Reread paragraph 21 of *My Diary from Here to There*. Then answer the questions.

2. How do the moves from one house to another impact Amada?

_____

_____

_____

3. How do you think the challenges of such a big move are impacting Amada's siblings?

_____

_____

Name _____

Prefixes over-, under-

▶ Complete the chart with other words that contain each prefix.

over–	under–
overcook	undercover

▶ Write sentences with words using the two prefixes.

_____

_____

_____

_____

_____

_____

Point of View

Point of view is who is telling the story. In the first-person point of view, the narrator is telling the story, using the pronouns *I*, *me*, and *we*. In the third-person point of view, the narrator is outside the story, using the pronouns *he*, *she*, and *they*.

> **Reread paragraph 1 of** *My Diary from Here to There*. **Then answer the questions.**

1. From what point of view is this story being told?

_____

2. Why do you think the author chooses this point of view to tell the story?

_____

_____

3. How does Amada's reaction to moving to Los Angeles compare to that of her brothers?

_____

_____

_____

_____

> **Reread paragraphs 19–20 of** *My Diary from Here to There*. **Then answer the question.**

4. Whose point of view are we reading when we read the letter from Papá? How do you know?

_____

_____

Name _____

Vowel + /r/ and Suffixes –y, –ly

> Read each sentence. Decide which word from the word box best completes the sentence and write it in the blank. Circle the letters in the word that make the vowel sound of / är/, /âr/, or /ir/. Does the word have a suffix of –y or –ly? Underline it.

prairie	sparkly	dearly	sparingly
dreary	unfairly	teary	scarcely
fearfully	rarely	sleepily	carelessly

1. When John's mother punished him, even though he didn't break the vase,

    she treated him _____ .

2. Pioneers used to travel across the _____ in covered wagons.

3. My older brother is so busy that I _____ see him.

4. The children were scared that there might be a monster in the closet,

    as they _____ opened the closet door.

5. It rained all morning and the clouds made the day dark and _____ .

6. When my sister lost her favorite toy, she was _____ and sad.

7. The princess wore a _____ gown to the ball.

8. A mother _____ loves all of her children.

Name _____

Author's Craft

Author's craft is the language and techniques a writer uses to make their writing more interesting. Authors may use **figurative language** to describe events and characters. They may also use **literal language** to tell readers what is happening in a story.

▶ **Reread paragraphs 7–9 of *My Diary from Here to There*. Then answer the questions.**

1. What anecdote, or story by a character, is told?

_____

_____

2. Why does the author choose to have Michi tell an anecdote about her family here?

_____

_____

▶ **Reread paragraph 32 of *My Diary from Here to There*. Then answer the questions.**

3. Find examples of how the author's use of language contributes to voice.

_____

_____

_____

_____

4. Find an example in the text that shows how the author uses literal language to show her voice and engage readers.

_____

_____

_____

Name _____

More Vowel + /r/ Sounds /ûr/ /ôr/

> Read each sentence. Choose the word that best replaces the underlined word or words in each sentence and write it on the line. Does the word make an /ûr/ or /ôr/ sound? Circle the letters that stand for the sound.

burn	dirty	burst	world	sore
thirsty	current	board	search	course
return	pure	learn	thirteen	early
worn	worse	cure	record	sport

Sentence	Word	Sound
1. Please put the <u>soiled</u> clothes in the washing machine.	_____	/ûr/ /ôr/
2. The librarian says we have to <u>bring back</u> the books in two weeks.	_____	/ûr/ /ôr/
3. Cara's ankle was <u>aching</u> after soccer practice.	_____	/ûr/ /ôr/
4. The whole <u>neighborhood</u> will look for our lost dog.	_____	/ûr/ /ôr/
5. When it gets cold, we will <u>set fire</u> to the logs in our fireplace.	_____	/ûr/ /ôr/
6. Our <u>planet</u> is made up of land and water.	_____	/ûr/ /ôr/
7. Is it fun to <u>discover</u> new things by reading?	_____	/ûr/ /ôr/
8. The hot sun and sand of the Sahara Desert made the explorers <u>desire</u> water.	_____	/ûr/ /ôr/
9. Track and field is my favorite <u>athletic</u> game.	_____	/ûr/ /ôr/
10. Jacob's assignment was to write an <u>up-to-date</u> report on the volcanic eruption.	_____	/ûr/ /ôr/

Critical Vocabulary

You can use the words you learn from reading as you talk and write.

▶ **Use your understanding of the Critical Vocabulary words from *Prince Charming Misplaces His Bride* to help you finish each sentence.**

1. My brother **sulked** in his room because _____

_____

2. When I heard a **foreboding** click, I knew _____

_____

3. I felt my backbone get **rigid** when _____

_____

4. My hair is **disheveled** because _____

_____

5. Our new puppy gets **feisty** when _____

_____

6. What made the event really **elegant** was _____

_____

7. We felt **intimidated** by the other team because _____

_____

8. I **scowled** at my sister because _____

_____

Name _____

9. The **episode** with forgotten homework taught me _____

_____

10. The audience's **subdued** response showed _____

_____

▶ **Choose two of the Critical Vocabulary words and use them in a sentence.**

_____

_____

Point of View

The **point of view** of a story is told using first-person point of view or third-person point of view. When the story is told in first-person point of view, the narrator of the story is a character in the story. Readers can look for key words such as *I*, *me*, and *we* to signal first-person point of view. When a story is told in third-person point of view, the narrator is not in the story but is outside the story. Readers can look for key words such as *he*, *she*, *they* and character names to signal third-person point of view.

> Reread paragraph 13 of *Prince Charming Misplaces His Bride* to determine the point of view. Then answer the other questions.

1. What point of view does the author use in paragraph 13?

_____

_____

2. How do you know?

_____

_____

_____

> Reread page 261 and answer the question below.

3. How would the story be different if Frederic were the narrator?

_____

_____

_____

_____

_____

More Vowel + /r/ Sounds /ûr/ /ôr/

> worth   worn   worse   world   warn

1. Write three words from the box above with the same /r/ sound.

_____   _____   _____

> current   course   courage   cure

2. Write two words from the box above that have two syllables.

_____   _____

> worthwhile   further   thirteen

3. Write the word from the box above that is a number.

_____

> board   sport   world   afford

4. Which words from the word boxes make the same /ôr/ sound as the word *sore*? Write the words on the blanks and circle the letters that stand for the /ôr/ sound.

_____   _____   _____

_____   _____   _____

Prefixes sub-, fore-

> Complete the chart with other words that contain each prefix.

sub-	fore-
subtopic	foreground

> Write sentences with words using the two prefixes.

_____

_____

_____

_____

_____

_____

Name _____

Theme

The **theme** of a story is the main message, lesson, or moral of the text. Sometimes the theme is stated by the author. Other times, the theme is implied using details in the text. The reader is left to figure out the theme.

> Reread paragraphs 86–96 of *Prince Charming Misplaces His Bride* to determine the theme. Then answer the questions below.

1. What advice does Reginald give Frederic and in what way?

_____

_____

_____

_____

2. What message or lesson is the author trying to communicate?

_____

_____

_____

_____

3. How can you use this message and relate it to your everyday life?

_____

_____

_____

Text and Graphic Features

Text features can present important parts of a story. Different kinds of type such as boldface, italics, or capital letters may be used by an author to communicate something important to get the reader's attention. Authors may also use different types of punctuation, such as an exclamation point to express fear, excitement, or other emotions without using many words.

Graphic features are visuals such as illustrations, diagrams, maps, and speech bubbles that help explain ideas in a text.

> Revisit pages 246 and 247 in *Prince Charming Misplaces His Bride*. Then answer the question below.

1. How is the text written on both pages, and what do these text features tell the reader?

_____

_____

> Revisit page 253 in *Prince Charming Misplaces His Bride*. Then answer the question.

2. What details in the illustration help you understand the relationship between Ella and Frederic?

_____

_____

> Revisit page 258 in *Prince Charming Misplaces His Bride*. Then answer the question.

3. How does the text change on this page, and why does the author change it?

_____

_____

Name _____

Regular and Irregular Plurals

> Read each sentence. Decode the underlined nouns. Write the nouns in the plural on the line below.

1. The child took the book from the shelf.

_____

2. He has curly, red hair.

_____

3. Mary had her tooth pulled.

_____

4. The baby began to play with the toy.

_____

5. The plant attracted the butterfly.

_____

6. The man brought the box into the store.

_____

Name _____

Critical Vocabulary

You can use the words you learn from reading as you talk and write.

> **Use your understanding of the Critical Vocabulary words from *Smokejumpers to the Rescue* to support your answers to the questions below.**

1. Would you recommend a person who is **timid** work as a smokejumper? Why or why not?

_____

_____

_____

2. What are some strenuous tasks that smokejumpers must perform in their job?

_____

_____

_____

> **Write a sentence for each of the Critical Vocabulary words.**

_____

_____

_____

_____

Name _____

Text Structure

The way authors organize information in a text is called its **text structure**. Authors choose a text structure that highlights their reason for writing.

If the author wants to . . .	the text structure may be . . .
tell events in the order they happened	chronological order or in sequence
explain what happened and why	cause and effect
show how things are alike and different	compare and contrast

Sometimes authors organize information to explain a problem and tell how to fix it. In a problem-and-solution text structure, the writer gives details about a problem and then describes how to correct it or deal with it.

> Revisit *Smokejumpers to the Rescue!* to determine the text structure.

1. What text structure does the author use?

_____

2. Give examples of a problem and solution within the text.

_____

_____

_____

_____

3. What other text structure did you find? Why did the author use it?

_____

_____

Elements of Drama

Stories are written in paragraphs that connect to form chapters. Poems are written in lines that connect to form stanzas. How is a play different?

A drama, or **play**, is a story that is meant to be performed for an audience. The **script** of a play tells directors, actors, and backstage helpers exactly how to perform the play on stage.

- The **cast of characters** is a list of people, animals, or other beings in the play. It usually appears at the beginning of the script.

- **Stage directions** appear throughout a script and are usually in italic type. Stage directions may describe the setting for each scene, the way a character should say a line, or when characters enter, exit, or move.

- The words characters say to each other are called **dialogue**. Each line of dialogue begins with the name of the character who should say those words. Dialogue builds to reveal the plot of the play.

> **Review page 276 of _Perseus and the Fall of Medusa_. Then answer the question.**

1. How does the information in the cast of characters help you think about what might happen in the play?

_____

_____

> **Reread lines 9–18 of _Perseus and the Fall of Medusa_. Then answer the questions.**

2. What do the stage directions show about how each character should speak?

_____

3. How does the dialogue reveal the problem Perseus faces?

_____

_____

Suffixes –able, –ible

> Complete the chart with other words that contain each suffix.

–able	–ible

> Write sentences with words using the two suffixes.

_____

_____

_____

_____

_____

Figurative Language

Figurative language is the use of words or phrases to suggest more than what the words actually mean. Figurative language may help readers understand an idea by reminding them of a well-known person or thing. It may make comparisons or create strong images. Using figurative language helps readers see ideas in new ways.

Type	What It Is	Example
Allusion	A brief reference to a person, place, thing, or idea from literature or history; many allusions refer to myths	*It was no surprise that a ship named Poseidon sank to the bottom of the sea!*
Simile	The use of the words *like* or *as* to compare one thing to another thing	*The anger in Eugene's eyes burned as bright as coals.*
Imagery	A description that creates a strong image in the reader's mind or appeals to other senses	*The worn wooden door was cracked and splintered.*

> **Reread lines 22–35 from *Perseus and the Fall of Medusa* and answer the questions.**

1. What are some examples of imagery in the text? How do they help readers?

_____

_____

2. Which stage direction includes a simile? What does this comparison help you imagine?

_____

_____

> **Reread page 284 of *Perseus and the Fall of Medusa* to identify the use of figurative language.**

3. The *Odyssey* is a well-known Greek poem. What comparison does the author make to this poem?

_____

_____

Name _____

Spelling Word Sort: Adding -ed or -ing

> Choose three spelling words from the word box that follow each rule.
Write them on the lines in the correct boxes.

striped	surprising	dripped	begged
skipped	handled	forgetting	dancing
traced	rising	winning	spinning

Add –ed: drop the final e before adding –ed	_____ _____ _____
Add –ed: double the final consonant before adding –ed	_____ _____ _____
Add –ing: drop the final e before adding –ing	_____ _____ _____
Add –ing: double the final consonant before adding –ing	_____ _____ _____

Critical Vocabulary

You can use the words you learn from reading as you talk and write.

▶ **Use details from *The Battle of the Alamo* to support your answers to the questions below. Then use the Critical Vocabulary words as you talk with a partner about your answers.**

1. Tell about a time one of your favorite book or movie characters **surrendered** to an enemy.

_____

2. How would you describe a **rebellion**?

_____

3. How would you feel if something made you **furious**?

_____

4. Do you think it would be good to have a leader who was a **tyrant**?

_____

5. If you go to the movie theater **occasionally**, how often do you go?

_____

6. Where is the place where you feel the most **secure**? Explain.

_____

▶ **Write a sentence using two Critical Vocabulary words below.**

_____

_____

Name _____

Central Idea

The **central idea** of a text is the big idea, or the main idea, that readers should take away with them after reading the text. The central idea is supported by details, such as facts, examples, and descriptions. Readers **evaluate** details to determine key ideas.

> **Reread paragraphs 5–8 in *The Battle of the Alamo*. Then complete the exercise below.**

1. Determine the central, or main, idea that is introduced for this nonfiction narrative.

_____

_____

_____

> **Reread page 299 in *The Battle of the Alamo*. Then complete the exercises below.**

2. Consider the central, or main, idea as you answer this question. What are some of the hardest decisions that the people inside the Alamo have to make?

_____

_____

_____

3. What details on page 299 support the central, or main, idea?

_____

_____

_____

_____

_____

Suffixes –en, –ic

> Complete the chart with other words that contain each suffix.

–en	–ic

> Write sentences with words using the two suffixes.

_____

_____

_____

_____

_____

Name _____

Text Structure

Information in nonfiction texts can be organized in a number of ways. Identifying the **text structure**, or the way in which the information is organized, can help you better understand a nonfiction text.

> **Reread paragraph 5 to identify the cause-and-effect text structure. Then answer the questions about *The Battle of the Alamo*.**

1. What is the effect of Santa Anna's thoughts about the new constitution?

_____

_____

2. What is the effect of these new laws?

_____

> **Reread paragraph 22 and answer the questions.**

3. What happens when William Travis sees Santa Anna and the red flag he raises?

_____

4. How does recognizing the cause-and-effect text structure of this event help you better understand the narrative?

_____

_____

_____

> **Reread paragraphs 42–44 to determine the cause-and-effect text structure.**

5. What is the effect of Travis drawing a line in the sand with his sword?

_____

_____

Recognize Root Words: Suffixes -able, -ible

▶ Complete the crossword puzzle with words with suffixes *–able* and *–ible*.

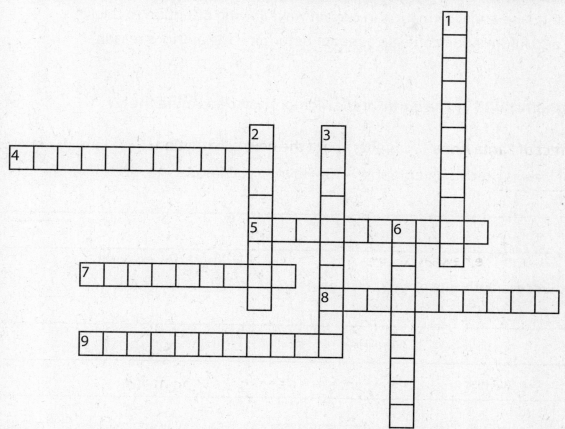

Across

4. car with a folding or detachable top

_____

5. difficult to believe, extraordinary

_____

7. a person who is pleasant and

charming _____

8. real; able to be true _____

9. Providing ease and relaxation; free from

pain _____

Down

1. able to be known beforehand

_____

2. very bad; awful

_____

3. inexpensive; reasonably priced

_____

6. something that can't be seen

_____

Name _____

Author's Purpose

Author's purpose is the author's reason for writing. Based on his or her purpose, an author uses language and information in certain ways. Paying attention to this use of language and information can help a reader determine the author's reason for writing.

> Reread paragraphs 9–15 in *The Battle of the Alamo*. Then determine the author's purpose.

1. What point of view is used in paragraphs 9–15? How do you know?

   _____

   _____

2. Why do you think the author uses this point of view?

   _____

   _____

> Think about *The Battle of the Alamo*. Then answer the questions.

3. In the end, what purpose did the author have for writing this nonfiction narrative?

   _____

   _____

4. What elements did she use to meet her purpose?

   _____

   _____

   _____

Name _Victoria Lima_

(3)28, NOV, IYe, 2023

Decoding

Recognize Root Words

> Read each sentence. Underline the word that has a word ending of either *-ing* or *-ed*. Then write the root word on the line provided.

1. The squirrel buried the nuts in the ground. _bury_

2. Timothy scraped his knee when he fell off his bike. _scrape_

3. Lillian was so cold, she was shaking! _shake_

4. Roberto tried to do his best on the test. _trie_

5. Do you like to go hiking? _hike_

6. Every week, my family goes shopping for groceries. _shop_

7. Jermaine scratched the spot where a mosquito bit him. _scratch_

8. Are you good at adding numbers together? _add_

9. My puppy is happy to be outside digging in our yard. _dig_

10. My dad thinks that riding a train to work is very convenient. _ride_

Grade 4

95

Module 5 • Week 1

Name ___Victoria Dima___ @28 INOVITUK, 2023

Critical Vocabulary

You can use the words you learn from reading as you talk and write.

> **Use your understanding of the Critical Vocabulary words to support your answers to the questions below. Then use the words as you talk with a partner about your answers.**

1. What activity would you perform in a **dignified** manner?

The dignified soldier stand properly

2. What new technology has **stunned** you lately?

The I Phone 14 stunned me.

3. Why is it important to be a **polished** speaker?

So you don't mess up.

4. If you **regretted** something you had said, what could you do?

_____

_____

5. What comedy actor do you find **hysterical**?

_____

_____

6. How can you tell if a friend is an **observant** person?

_____

_____

Name _____

7. What is the best way to **flatter** you?

_____

_____

8. What would you do if your homework was **trampled**?

_____

_____

> **Write a sentence using two Critical Vocabulary words below.**

_____

_____

Name _____

Ideas and Support

When authors present their **ideas** in a nonfiction text, they must have **support**, or be backed up by reasons and evidence. A text can have different kinds of reasons and evidence.

- A **fact** is a statement that is true and can be proved. Authors also provide details and examples to prove their point.
- An **opinion** tells what someone feels or believes is true. It cannot be proved, but reasons or evidence provided with an opinion may make it seem true.

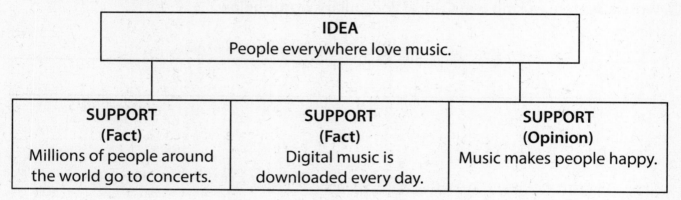

IDEA
People everywhere love music.

SUPPORT (Fact)	SUPPORT (Fact)	SUPPORT (Opinion)
Millions of people around the world go to concerts.	Digital music is downloaded every day.	Music makes people happy.

▶ **Reread paragraphs 17 and 18 in** *The Beatles Were Fab (and They Were Funny)* **and answer the question below.**

1. How do the authors support their idea that the Beatles were funny?

_____

_____

_____

▶ **Reread paragraphs 23 and 24 and answer the question below.**

2. How do the authors feel about the suddenly famous Beatles? Is this a fact or an opinion?

_____

_____

Recognize Root Words in Multisyllabic Words

> ▸ **Read each sentence. Write the root word of the underlined word on the line.**

1. The football team is <u>undefeated</u> this season. _____

2. We <u>repainted</u> my room a bright blue. _____

3. His grades are <u>improving</u> because he has been working hard. _____

4. My favorite magic trick is the <u>disappearing</u> coin. _____

5. My mom <u>disinfected</u> my cut before putting on the bandage. _____

6. My grandmother <u>subscribed</u> to her favorite magazine for an entire year. _____

7. I found the movie about airplanes to be quite <u>uninteresting</u>. _____

8. I am <u>rethinking</u> my decision to go to the park with my friends. _____

Name _____

Suffixes –ity, –ty

A **suffix** is a word part added to the end of a base word that changes the meaning of the word. When the suffixes *–ity* and *–ty* are placed at the end of a base word, its part of speech changes.

> **Complete the chart with words that contain suffixes** *–ity* **and** *–ty.*

–ity	–ty

> **Choose 3 words from the chart and write a sentence for each word.**

_____

_____

_____

_____

_____

_____

_____

_____

Text Structure

Text structure is how authors organize their texts. Sometimes a selection has several different text structures. In selections with multiple types of text structures, the authors organize parts of their texts based on what will best get their ideas across.

Text Structures	Purpose
Comparison/Contrast	To tell how ideas or topics are alike and different
Cause/Effect	To explain what happens and why
Chronological	To tell events in order of how they happened
Problem/Solution	To explain a problem and tell how it is solved

> Reread paragraphs 10–13 to analyze *The Beatles Were Fab (and They Were Funny)* for its structure. Then answer the questions.

1. How is this part of the text organized?

_____

_____

2. What clues do the authors include to show the text structure?

_____

_____

3. How does knowing the text's structure help you understand the author's purpose for writing?

_____

_____

Name _____

Figurative Language

Authors use **figurative language** to compare, exaggerate, or mean something different from what the reader would expect. **Idioms** or phrases that mean something different from what the individual words mean, are one type of figurative language. Authors may also use **descriptive language** and **sensory words** to appeal to readers' senses. These vivid details help readers picture what is happening in the text.

> ▶ **Reread paragraph 5 in *The Beatles Were Fab (and They Were Funny)*. Answer the question below.**

1. How do the authors use figurative language in paragraph 5? Explain.

_____

_____

_____

_____

_____

> ▶ **Reread paragraph 26 to identify the authors' use of figurative language and sensory words. Then answer the questions.**

2. What figurative language do the authors use to describe Beatlemania during the 1964 tour?

_____

_____

3. What descriptive language helps you visualize the places the Beatles played during their concerts?

_____

_____

Final Long e

> **Read each sentence. Underline the word that has a final long *e* sound.
Then circle the letter or letters that stand for that sound.**

1. My teacher put a smiley face sticker on my book report.

2. The wooden doors in the old house are squeaky.

3. My favorite breed of dog is a collie.

4. Do you like the sound of a canary singing?

5. Charlie plays many sports and is a talented athlete.

6. My grandmother makes a delicious beef and barley soup.

7. The food was so spicy that it made my eyes water!

8. It is important to eat healthy foods like fruits and vegetables.

9. The apple pie had a flaky crust.

10. This book is about a pixie who lives in an enchanted forest.

Name _____

Critical Vocabulary

You can use the words you learn from reading as you talk and write.

> **Use your understanding of the Critical Vocabulary words to support your answers to the questions below. Then use the words as you talk with a partner about your answers.**

1. What might a **curator** at a history museum do?

_____

_____

2. When you take a picture, do you focus on the object in the **foreground** or the **background**? Explain.

_____

_____

> **Write a sentence using at least two of the Critical Vocabulary words below.**

_____

_____

_____

_____

_____

_____

Name _____

Central Idea

Videos, like text selections, can also have a **central**, or main, **idea**. A central idea is what the video is about. Details can be found throughout the video that support the central idea. A central idea and details can be found in what the speakers say and in the images in the video.

> **Have students answer the following questions about the video.**

1. What video clues tell you the central, or main, idea of this video?

_____

_____

_____

_____

2. What do you think is the central, or main, idea of this video? How can you tell?

_____

_____

_____

_____

3. What are some details, facts, or evidence that supports the central, or main, idea?

_____

_____

_____

_____

Name _____

Final Long *e* in Multisyllabic Words

▶ Read the words in the box. Then read each sentence. Find a word in the box that makes the most sense in the sentence. Write the word on the line and underline the letters that stand for the long *e* sound. Use each word one time. Some words will not be used.

unhappy	varsity
birdie	parsley
activity	auntie
abbey	Academy
baggie	ability

1. When I was packing my lunch, I put the sandwich in a _____ .

2. My brother was very excited when he made the _____ team.

3. Her _____ to play the guitar is amazing.

4. My mom added _____ to the chicken soup.

5. Jose's _____ lives in the state of Montana.

6. When Lola lost her favorite book, she was very _____ .

7. My older brother and sister go to school at Lane _____ .

8. Physical _____ is important for living a healthy life.

Name _____

Critical Vocabulary

You can use the words you learn from reading as you talk and write.

> Use your understanding of the Critical Vocabulary words to support your answers to the questions below. Then use the words as you talk with a partner about your answers.

1. Which musician in a marching band provides the **rhythmic** beat?

_____

_____

2. Who do you know that has a **distinctive** voice?

_____

_____

3. What characteristic would you **highlight** as an example of your personality?

_____

_____

4. Do you think elevators will ever be **horizontal**?

_____

_____

> Write a sentence using two Critical Vocabulary words below.

_____

_____

Name _Victouria Pino ③ 12/Dec/tuer 2023_

Text Structure

The way a text is organized helps you understand how an author's ideas are connected to one another. Authors use an organization, or **text structure**, that best highlights or emphasizes their central, or main, idea.

An author may begin with a familiar idea, and then tell how other ideas are alike and different. This organization is a **compare-and-contrast** text structure. Other text structures include **cause-and-effect** and **problem-solution**.

▶ **Reread paragraph 6 in** *Let's Dance Around the World*. **Then answer the following questions.**

1. What text structure does the author use in this part of the text? Why?

   Comparison/Contrast, because they are comparing Break dancing and tap

2. How are tap and break dancing alike? How do they differ from folk dancing?

   Their are alike Because they Both use dance. folk dancing is different because its done by 2 people.

▶ **Reread paragraphs 11–12 and then answer the following questions.**

3. How are the limbo and the Brazilian capoeira different from one another? How are they similar?

   The limbo and the Capoeira are different because capoeira does dance and martial arts and limbo is competive, their are alike Because they both listen to music.

Suffixes –er, –or, –ist

When you see a word with the suffix –er, –or, and –ist, look for a base word as a clue to the meaning of the word. The words *sailor*, *hunter*, and *typist* are made up of a base word and a suffix.

▶ Complete the chart with other words that contain the suffixes –er, –or, and –ist. (Hint: think of job titles to help you come up with words.)

–er	–or	–ist

▶ Choose 3 words from the chart and write a sentence for each word.

_____

_____

_____

_____

_____

_____

_____

Name _____

Text and Graphic Features

Informational texts often include **visuals**, such as charts, diagrams, photographs, and illustrations. Pictures and other kinds of visuals add to a reader's understanding of a written text. They present new information that may be hard to explain using just words. Labeled photographs or illustrations can show important details that make the meaning of a text clearer.

> **Reread paragraph 5 in *Let's Dance Around the World*. Then answer the following questions.**

1. How does the photograph connect to the text?

_____

_____

2. How does the photograph add to your understanding of the ideas in the text?

_____

_____

> **Reread page 353 and answer the following questions.**

3. What text or graphic features are shown on this page?

_____

_____

4. What new information do you learn from the photos that is not in the text?

_____

_____

Recognize Root Words

> Read each sentence. Underline the word that has a word ending of *-er*, *-est*, *-ed*, or *-es* added to a root word. Then write the root word on the line provided.

1. We picked the fluffiest kitten in the litter. <u>fluffly pick</u>

2. Do you like to eat fried chicken? <u>frie chick</u>

3. The daisies look delightful! <u>daisy</u>

4. Today is windier than yesterday. <u>wind</u>

5. A good student always tries his or her best. <u>trie</u>

6. My uncle carried the heaviest box. <u>carry heavy</u>

7. We enjoyed riding the ponies at the fair. <u>enjoy pony</u>

8. My grandparents have been married for 50 years. <u>marry</u>

9. What kind of stories do you like to read? <u>story</u>

10. She is much happier when she gets a good night's sleep. <u>happy</u>

Name _____

Critical Vocabulary

You can use the words you learn from reading as you talk and write.

▶ **Use your understanding of the Critical Vocabulary words to support your answers to the questions below. Then use the words as you talk with a partner about your answers.**

1. How much homework is **necessary** for a fourth grader?

   One of the fourth grade teacher gave us a sheet of paper.

2. What kind of jacket gives you **unsurpassed** protection in a snowstorm?

   I kindoe get unsurpassed in a snowstom.

3. What might a toddler do to cause a **stir** in a supermarket?

   She might get excitement

4. What is an **extraordinarily** good book you might recommend?

   A extraordinarily book is cinerll

5. What's the best thing about **cruising** on a boat?

   We went cruising in a lake

6. What happens to the surface of a lake when something heavy **plunges** into it?

   It starts to plung.

▶ **Write a sentence using two Critical Vocabulary words below.**

   Sometimes I get unsurpassed dad cause a stir.

Theme

The **theme** of a poem is its main message or lesson. Both poets and authors of fictional texts often include themes in their writing. The theme of a poem may be stated, but often the theme is implied by the details the poet uses.

> **Reread pages 361–365 in *The Art of Poetry* and answer the question below.**

1. What is the theme of the first three poems in this selection?

_____

_____

_____

_____

> **Reread pages 368–369 in *The Art of Poetry* and answer the questions below.**

2. What is the theme of the poem?

_____

3. What message is the poet trying to send to the reader?

_____

_____

_____

> **Reread pages 368–370 in *The Art of Poetry* and answer the questions below.**

4. What common themes do you find in the poems written by Francisco X. Alarcón? What is his message to the reader?

_____

_____

Name _____

Words with /k/, /ng/, and /kw/

▶ **Read each sentence. Find the word that includes a /k/, /kw/, or /ng/ sound. Underline the letter or group of letters that stand for that sound. After the sentence, underline "/k/ Sound", "/kw/ Sound", or "/ng/ Sound".**

1. My brother is younger than me.
    /k/ Sound   /kw/ Sound   /ng/ Sound

2. After spending the day at the beach, Jessie's face was dotted with freckles.
    /k/ Sound   /kw/ Sound   /ng/ Sound

3. Louis is very athletic, and he plays many different sports.
    /k/ Sound   /kw/ Sound   /ng/ Sound

4. Maria goes to the library frequently because she loves to read.
    /k/ Sound   /kw/ Sound   /ng/ Sound

5. What do you wear when you go outside on a brisk day?
    /k/ Sound   /kw/ Sound   /ng/ Sound

6. Elizabeth squealed with delight when she saw the gift inside the box.
    /k/ Sound   /kw/ Sound   /ng/ Sound

7. The little duckling waddled behind its mother on the way to the pond.
    /k/ Sound   /kw/ Sound   /ng/ Sound

8. As she got into bed, Sandra wrapped the fuzzy blanket around her.
    /k/ Sound   /kw/ Sound   /ng/ Sound

9. Fire fighters are heroes because they risk their lives to save people who are in danger.
    /k/ Sound   /kw/ Sound   /ng/ Sound

10. When we traveled through the mountains last summer, I enjoyed the scenic view.
    /k/ Sound   /kw/ Sound   /ng/ Sound

Critical Vocabulary

> Use your understanding of the Critical Vocabulary words from *The Mariana Trench* to support your answers to the questions below.

1. Why is the **summit** of Mount Everest famous?

_____

_____

2. What is something **vital** to the exploration of the ocean floor?

_____

_____

3. Why is a **submersible** vehicle useful to oceanographers?

_____

_____

4. What might you have seen in **prehistoric** times?

_____

_____

5. Where might you see a **trench**?

_____

_____

6. What are some things that are needed for living things to **thrive**?

_____

_____

7. How could a **remotely**-controlled vehicle help scientists explore the ocean?

_____

_____

8. How could you get a **glimpse** of deep sea creatures?

_____

_____

9. Would you drive an **autonomous** ocean vehicle? Why or why not?

_____

_____

▶ Choose two of the Critical Vocabulary words and use them in a sentence.

_____

_____

Greek Roots auto, bio, photo, graph

> Complete the chart with other words that contain the roots *auto*, *bio*, *photo*, and *graph*.

auto	bio	photo	graph

> Write a sentence for each word in the chart.

_____

_____

_____

_____

_____

_____

_____

_____

_____

_____

_____

_____

Name _____

Text Structure

The way information is arranged in a text is its **structure**.

- In a **chronological** text structure, events are told in the order they happen.

- A **problem-solution** structure describes a problem and how it is solved.

- A text with a **cause-effect** structure explains what happens and why.

- In a **comparison** text structure, authors tell how things are alike and different.

> Read paragraph 18 in *Mariana Trench,* and analyze the text structure. Read and answer the questions. Support your answers.

1. What is the structure of this part of the text?

_____

_____

_____

2. How does knowing the structure help you understand the central idea on this page?

_____

_____

3. What signal words helped you decide the structure?

_____

Text and Graphic Features

Text features help the reader attend to important details in a text.

- Sometimes writers use **boldface** or *italic* type to help readers attend to special or important words.

- Sometimes writers use pronunciation guides to help readers figure out how to pronounce difficult words or names of unfamiliar places.

Graphic features, such as photographs and maps, give the reader additional information about a topic.

▶ Read page 21 in *Mariana Trench*. Connect the text to the map. Then read and answer the question.

1. How does the map help you understand more about the text?

_____

_____

▶ Read paragraph 14 on page 27. Then read and answer the question. Support your answer.

2. Why do you think the author adds the pronunciation guide to this page?

_____

_____

3. Choose another graphic feature. Explain what it shows and why it is included.

_____

_____

_____

Name _____

Words with Final /j/ and /s/

▶ Read each sentence. Find the word that includes the final sound of /j/ or /s/.
Underline the letter or group of letters that stand for that sound. Below the
sentence, underline "Final /j/ Sound" or "Final /s/ Sound". Then, write the number
of syllables in the word on the line.

1. My mom likes to shop when items are on clearance.
   Final /j/   Final /s/   # of Syllables _____

2. I tried to convince my parents to let me go to the party.
   Final /j/   Final /s/   # of Syllables _____

3. A cold beverage is refreshing on a hot day.
   Final /j/   Final /s/   # of Syllables _____

4. The audience applauded at the end of the concert.
   Final /j/   Final /s/   # of Syllables _____

5. "Who ate all of my porridge?" Baby Bear asked.
   Final /j/   Final /s/   # of Syllables _____

6. What language do you speak?
   Final /j/   Final /s/   # of Syllables _____

7. As I climbed over the fence, I ripped my pants!
   Final /j/   Final /s/   # of Syllables _____

8. After playing outside, Leo had a smudge of dirt on his face.
   Final /j/   Final /s/   # of Syllables _____

9. Marathon runners have to train to run such a long distance.
   Final /j/   Final /s/   # of Syllables _____

10. Police officers and fire fighters need courage to help people in danger.
    Final /j/   Final /s/   # of Syllables _____

..

Critical Vocabulary

You can use the words you learn from reading as you talk and write.

> **Use your understanding of the Critical Vocabulary words from *Weird and Wondrous Rocks* to support your answers to the questions below. Then talk with a partner about your answers, using the Critical Vocabulary Words.**

1. Would you describe a fire that went out permanently as an **eternal** flame? Explain.

_____

_____

2. What is the **organic** matter that is keeping the eternal flame burning?

_____

_____

3. Must you travel to an exotic location to find something that is **intriguing**? Explain.

_____

_____

> **Use each of the Critical Vocabulary words in a sentence.**

_____

_____

_____

_____

_____

_____

Name _____

Text Structure

The way an author organizes information in a piece of writing is called **text structure**. The author uses an organizational system that brings attention to key ideas. An author may use a **cause-and-effect** text structure to explain why something happens. The **cause** is the reason something happens. The thing that happens is the **effect**.

▶ **Read page 37. Then answer the questions about the text structures in *Weird and Wondrous Rocks.***

1. What are two causes for the ringing in the rocks?

_____

_____

_____

2. What is the author's purpose in using cause and effect here?

_____

▶ **Read page 40 and answer the questions.**

3. What mystery do scientists want to solve in Death Valley National Park?

_____

4. What do the scientists do to solve the mystery?

_____

_____

5. What text structure does the author use to organize information about the mystery?

_____

Words with Final /j/ and /s/

> Read each sentence. Find the word that includes the final sound of /j/ or /s/.
Underline the letter or group of letters that stand for that sound. After the
sentence, underline "Final /j/ Sound" or "Final /s/ Sound". Then, write the number
of syllables in the word.

1. The Pilgrims spent a lot of time preparing for their voyage.
   Final /j/   Final /s/   # of Syllables _____

2. It is important to turn off lights to reduce the use of electricity.
   Final /j/   Final /s/   # of Syllables _____

3. Joshua saved his allowance for six months to buy the bicycle.
   Final /j/   Final /s/   # of Syllables _____

4. Solving the multiplication problem was a big challenge for Alex.
   Final /j/   Final /s/   # of Syllables _____

5. Were you able to find a good reference for your report?
   Final /j/   Final /s/   # of Syllables _____

6. The nurse placed a bandage on my arm after I hurt myself.
   Final /j/   Final /s/   # of Syllables _____

7. What an amazing ballet performance!
   Final /j/   Final /s/   # of Syllables _____

8. My mom likes to use a lot of spice in her cooking.
   Final /j/   Final /s/   # of Syllables _____

9. "What a strange little robot!" the princess exclaimed.
   Final /j/   Final /s/   # of Syllables _____

10. I heard the sirens of the ambulance as it rushed to the hospital.
    Final /j/   Final /s/   # of Syllables _____

Critical Vocabulary

You can use the words you learn from reading as you talk and write.

> Use your understanding of the Critical Vocabulary words to support your answers to the questions below. Then talk with a partner about your answers, using the Critical Vocabulary words.

1. Why is it challenging to explore the **core** of the Mariana Trench? Explain.

_____

_____

2. How might the wind's **wrath** cause a **collision** during a thunderstorm?

_____

_____

3. If a person had many **diverse** activities to choose from, would that person be **idle**? Why or why not?

_____

_____

4. Why is it difficult to **fathom** the size of the universe?

_____

> Choose two of the Critical Vocabulary words and use them in a sentence.

_____

_____

_____

_____

_____

Author's Craft

Author's craft is the techniques an author uses to make his or her writing unique.
Voice is an author's style of writing. An author's voice comes across in the words he
or she writes. Voice reveals the author's attitudes and feelings about a topic. In
poetry, we hear the author's voice in the **figurative language** and **imagery** used.

▶ **Read the poem "The Great Barrier Reef" on page 49. Then answer the question.**

1. What words tell how the poet feels about the Great Barrier Reef? Cite evidence
   from the poem to show how his voice comes through.

   _____

   _____

▶ **Read the poem "Mount Everest" on page 51. Then answer the question.**

2. How does the poet use imagery to tell you about the experience of climbing
   Mount Everest?

   _____

   _____

3. Write a few sentences or a poem about a place you have visited. Use figurative
   language and imagery to show your author's voice.

   _____

   _____

   _____

   _____

Name _____

Suffixes –ness, –ment

The suffixes –*ness* and –*ment* can be added to base words to change the meaning of the word.

| fair | lovely | enjoy | replace |

> Complete the chart by choosing a word from the box above and adding either –*ness* or –*ment* to create new words.

–ness	–ment

> Write a sentence for each word in the chart.

_____

_____

_____

_____

_____

_____

_____

_____

_____

Elements of Poetry

Poems are usually arranged in lines that form stanzas. A **stanza**, or verse, is a group of **lines** in a poem that go together. Like a paragraph, a stanza often tells about one main idea.

Poems have a unique way of describing things. Personification is one of these ways. When a human quality is given to an animal or object, this is called **personification**.

> **Read "The Mariana Trench" on page 50 in** *Nature's Wonders*. **Then answer the questions.**

1. How many stanzas are there in "The Mariana Trench"? Which stanza contains personification? What thing acts as humans do?

   _____

   _____

> **Read "Mount Everest" on page 51 in** *Nature's Wonders*. **Then answer the questions.**

2. What is the subject of the poem?

   _____

3. How is the poem arranged?

   _____

   _____

4. What is the effect of this arrangement?

   _____

   _____

Name _____

Prefixes *re-*, *un-*, and *dis-* in multisyllabic words

> Read each sentence. Choose a word from the word box to complete each sentence. Write the word on the line. After writing the word, circle the prefix.

re–	un–	dis–
recreate	unpack	discomfort
refasten	uncommon	dislike
recover	unexpected	disagree

1. Jenna couldn't wait to _____ her suitcase after her vacation.

2. My mom used a needle and thread to _____ the button.

3. I _____ the taste of broccoli.

4. Caleb used the key to _____ the door.

5. The artist tried to _____ the beauty of the sunset in his painting.

6. Becca will sleep until noon on the weekend to _____ from a busy week.

7. Malik felt a lot of _____ after he fell off his bike.

8. Lila looked at the _____ present with excitement.

Name _____

Critical Vocabulary

You can use the words you learn from reading as you talk and write.

> Use your understanding of the Critical Vocabulary words to answer the questions below. Then talk with a partner about your answers, using the Critical Vocabulary words.

1. If you saw something that **shattered**, what would it look like?

_____

2. How would you describe a mountain that is **eroding**?

_____

3. How would **sentries** at an important building behave?

_____

4. How would you feel if you stood before a **chasm**?

_____

5. Think of something that **glistens**. How does it look?

_____

6. What would happen if you tried to move an object that was **embedded** in rock? Explain.

_____

> Choose two of the Critical Vocabulary words and use each in a sentence.

_____

_____

Ideas and Support

Some authors write to explain or describe something. Others want to convince you of something. In every case, the writer wants to share an idea.

Good writers **support**, or back up, their ideas with reasons and evidence. Authors use different kinds of reasons and evidence, such as the following:

- **Facts** are statements that are true and can be proved.
- **Opinions** tell what someone feels or believes. Opinions cannot be proved.
- **Examples** are a person, thing, or event that shows the author's point.

> **Read pages 61–62 in *Grand Canyon* and answer the questions.**

1. How does the author use evidence to support the ideas presented about the Havasupai Indians?

_____

_____

_____

2. What evidence supports the idea that the layers of rock on the trail have been around for millions of years?

_____

_____

_____

_____

3. Write a sentence that states a fact. Then write a sentence that states an opinion.

_____

_____

Name _____

Name _____

Prefix inter–

The prefix *inter*– means "between" or "among."

> Complete the web with words that contain the prefix *inter*–.

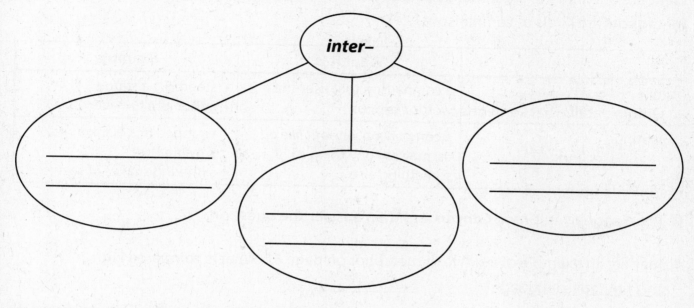

> Write a sentence for each word in the web.

_____

_____

_____

_____

_____

_____

_____

_____

Grade 4
© Houghton Mifflin Harcourt Publishing Company. All rights reserved.

137

Module 6 • Week 3

Name _____

Simile and Metaphor

Authors describe places or events so that readers can create pictures in their minds. The pictures or images help a reader to better understand a text. Often descriptions compare one thing to something else that readers are familiar with. **Similes** and **metaphors** are kinds of comparisons.

	What It Is	Example
simile	a comparison that uses the words *like* or *as*	• stood <u>like</u> a statue • <u>as</u> hot <u>as</u> a furnace
metaphor	a comparison without *like* or *as*; may say one thing is something else	• wrapped in a blanket of sunshine • slithering snakes of seaweed

> **Read page 61 in *Grand Canyon* and then answer the question.**

1. Identify an example of a simile or metaphor on page 61. What is compared with this figurative language?

   _____

   _____

   _____

2. Write an example of a simile you might use to describe something about the Grand Canyon.

   _____

   _____

   _____

3. Write an example of a metaphor you might use to describe something about the Grand Canyon.

   _____

   _____

Prefixes *re-*, *un-*, and *dis-* in multisyllabic words

> Read each sentence. Find the word that includes a prefix of *re-*, *un-*, or *dis-*, and underline it. After each sentence, circle the kind of prefix you see in the word you underlined.

1. Luke's baseball team was undefeated throughout the whole season.

    re–   un–   dis–

2. Latisha felt terrible about the disagreement with her best friend.

    re–   un–   dis–

3. Ramone felt very unsure on his first day of school.

    re–   un–   dis–

4. I had to rewrite my book report so it wouldn't have any mistakes.

    re–   un–   dis–

5. The school nurse used soap and water to disinfect the cut on my elbow.

    re–   un–   dis–

6. We stopped at a gas station on the highway to refuel the car.

    re–   un–   dis–

7. My mom put the leftover meat into the oven to reheat it for dinner.

    re–   un–   dis–

8. My dad decided to discontinue our membership to the zoo.

    re–   un–   dis–

9. Manuel is confident and unafraid in new situations.

    re–   un–   dis–

10. Alyssa had to remake the brownies for the bake sale because we ate the first batch.

    re–   un–   dis–

Name _____

Author's Craft

Remind students that when authors use descriptive language, they are trying to appeal to the readers' senses. Authors may also use vivid details to help readers picture what is happening in the text. The way an author uses language is known as the author's **voice** or style of writing.

> **Read pages 59–60 and answer the questions.**

1. On page 59, what are two examples of how the author uses descriptive language to help readers picture the view of the Grand Canyon?

_____

_____

_____

_____

2. On page 60, how does the author use sensory language to help you visualize what is happening in the text?

_____

_____

_____

_____

_____

> **Read paragraph 10 on page 63 and answer the question.**

3. What words does the author use that help you see how lizards act in the Canyon?

_____

_____

Name _____

Suffixes –ful, –less, –ness, –ment

▷ **Read each sentence. Choose a word from the word box that correctly completes each sentence. Write the word on the line.**

–ful	–less	–ness	–ment
wasteful	spotless	weakness	treatment
truthful	endless	dampness	enjoyment
cheerful	flawless	closeness	pavement

1. The house was _____ after we cleaned it.

2. The little boy skinned his knee on the _____ .

3. Grandmother is always _____ when we visit.

4. The _____ of the air made me shiver.

5. The train seemed _____ as we waited for it to pass.

6. When we recycle things we have used, we are not _____ .

7. The children got _____ from visiting the zoo.

8. The _____ of his mother comforted the crying baby.

Critical Vocabulary

You can use the words you learn from reading as you talk and write.

▶ **Use your understanding of the Critical Vocabulary words from *Thunder Rose* to support your answers to the questions below.**

1. What could you do to show that you are **partial** to something?

_____

_____

2. How does Tater's **disposition** change when Rose hums her tune?

_____

_____

3. What things might an Olympic athlete **vividly recall**?

_____

_____

4. What actions show that Rose is **resourceful**?

_____

_____

5. What did Rose do that **accentuated** her capture of Jesse Baines and his gang?

_____

_____

6. What kind of thing have you seen that you would call **commendable**?

_____

_____

Name _____

7. What types of things can cause **devastation**?

_____

_____

8. What places or things might display **splendor**? Explain.

_____

_____

> **Choose two of the Critical Vocabulary words and use them in a sentence.**

_____

Name _____

Figurative Language

Authors use **figurative language** to achieve specific purposes, such as to invoke a feeling or appeal to the senses. Authors may use figurative language to make a comparison, to exaggerate, or to make a point.

> **Reread paragraph 8 of *Thunder Rose*.**

1. What does the phrase "rattling the rafters" mean?

_____

_____

2. What kind of figurative language is this? Why?

_____

> **Reread paragraph 9 and answer the questions.**

3. What simile does the author use?

_____

4. Why is this comparison a good choice to describe Rose?

_____

5. What exaggeration, or hyperbole, does the author use?

_____

> **Reread paragraph 11 of *Thunder Rose*.**

6. What sensory words does the author use to describe where Rose lives? To which senses do these words appeal?

_____

Name _____

Suffixes –*ful*, –*less*, –*ness*, –*ment*

> Read the clue. Choose a word from the word box below and combine it with the suffix –*ful*, –*less*, –*ness*, or –*ment* to fit the clue.

peace	rest	weak	pave
color	move	use	neat

1. Unable to stay at rest: _____

2. Having bright colors: _____

3. The act of moving: _____

4. A state of having no strength: _____

5. Full of peace: _____

6. Not having any use: _____

7. A state of tidiness: _____

8. The hard surface of a road or street: _____

> Read each sentence. Write the correct word to complete it.

1. If the kitchen looks neat and clean, it is _____ .
  wasteful   spotless

2. When a person tells exactly what happened in an event, the person is

  being _____ .
    cheerful   truthful

Name _____

Suffix –ion

> Use what you know about the suffix *–ion* to answer the questions below.

1. If you gave someone directions, what did you do?

_____

_____

2. When might you need to take action at school?

_____

_____

3. If you were told to make a selection of something, what would you do?

_____

_____

4. Why might someone feel bad if they received a rejection?

_____

_____

5. What kinds of decorations would you see on your favorite holiday?

_____

_____

Name _____

Characters

Characters are the people and animals in a story. Readers should ask questions about the characters as they read. Here are some examples of questions you might ask:

- What does the character say?
- How does the character think and act?
- How does the character interact with others?
- How does the character change?

> **Read page 90 of *Thunder Rose* and answer the question.**

1. How does Tater change as a result of his interaction with Rose? Give examples from the text.

_____

_____

> **Use page 95 of *Thunder Rose* to answer the questions below.**

2. How does Rose react to the approaching tornadoes?

_____

3. How does her reaction to the approaching tornadoes compare to her reaction to the steer stampede earlier?

_____

_____

_____

4. Make a list of words that characterize Rose's character.

_____

Adages and Proverbs

Adages and proverbs are types of common expressions and sayings that have meanings beyond what can be understood by their individual words.

An **adage** is a short statement that express a general truth or advice.

A **proverb** is a short saying that usually has been around for centuries. It states a truth based on common sense or experiences.

> **Use paragraph 35 of *Thunder Rose* to answer the questions below.**

1. What does the adage "as thunder follows lightning, and sun follows rain" mean in this tall tale?

   _____

   _____

   _____

   _____

   _____

2. Why might the author have chosen this adage to end *Thunder Rose*?

   _____

   _____

   _____

3. Which of these sayings are adages or proverbs? Circle the adages and proverbs.

   Look before you leap.

   The clock strikes midnight.

   Always get plenty of sleep.

   The early bird gets the worm.

   Absence makes the heart grow fonder.

Name _____

Fill in the Blank: VCCV Pattern

> Read the sentence. Choose a word from the box on the right that correctly completes the sentence. Write the word in the blank.

1. Charlie had collected so many stamps, it seemed like he had a

    _____ of them.

2. Juanita asked if she could _____ my book because she liked the pretty cover.

3. We are going to be late because all of the cars on the road have

    caused a lot of _____ .

4. Tina was excited because her family was going to visit the

    Grand _____ .

5. After dinner, Alex wanted to open his _____ cookie to find out what was written inside.

6. Despite being trapped on the mountain without food or water,

    the hikers were able to _____ for over a week.

7. Kayla's aunt put the pretty _____ she drew up on the refrigerator.

8. Airplanes have a very big _____ , which helps them stay in the sky.

million
collect
lumber
pepper
plastic
borrow
support
thirty
perfect
attend
canyon
traffic
fortune
danger
soccer
engine
picture
survive
seldom
effort

Name _____

Critical Vocabulary

You can use the words you learn from reading as you talk and write.

> **Use your understanding of the Critical Vocabulary words from *In the Days of King Adobe* to support your answers to the questions below.**

1. Why might you be surprised if your **thrifty** neighbor went shopping every day? Explain.

_____

_____

2. What would you do if your aunt gave you a **generous** gift for your birthday?

_____

_____

3. Why might you receive an award for being a person of good **character**? Explain.

_____

_____

4. Would you be surprised if your kitten was **fascinated** by a ball of yarn? Why or why not?

_____

_____

> **Choose two of the Critical Vocabulary words and use them in a sentence.**

_____

_____

Critical Vocabulary

You can use the words you learn from reading as you talk and write.

> **Use your understanding of the Critical Vocabulary words from *A Pair of Tricksters* to support your answers to the questions below. Then talk with a partner about your answers, using the Critical Vocabulary words.**

1. Cacti live in dry places, but they are very **succulent** on the inside. What else is succulent on the inside?

   _____

   _____

2. If you **clamped** something, what did you do?

   _____

   _____

> **Write a sentence using each of the Critical Vocabulary words below.**

   _____

   _____

Figurative Language

Authors use language that helps readers picture a scene or feel a certain way. They may also use the sounds, such as alliteration and assonance, to connect ideas or to create phrases readers will remember. The chart shows examples of the kinds of figurative language authors may use.

Kind of Language	What It Is	Example
alliteration	repeating the beginning sound in words	*We could hear the rat-a-tat-tat of rain on the roof.*
assonance	repeating the vowel sound in words	*It's a treat to feel the heat.*

> **Reread page 120 of *Raven and Crayfish*.**

1. How does the author use alliteration in the text? Why?

_____

_____

_____

_____

2. How does the author use assonance, or repeated vowel sounds, in that phrase?

_____

_____

3. Why does the author repeat the alliteration at the end of the story?

_____

_____

4. Write a sentence using assonance or alliteration.

_____

Prefixes *mis-*, *pre-*, and *dis-*

> Use what you know about the prefixes to answer the questions below. Then use the underlined words as you talk with a partner about your answers.

1. What might happen if you <u>misbehave</u> at school?

_____

_____

2. Why might you need to <u>presoak</u> your clothes?

_____

_____

3. What would happen to a runner who was <u>disqualified</u> from a race?

_____

_____

> Write a sentence using each of the underlined words.

_____

_____

_____

Name _____

Characters

Literary elements are the pieces that make up a story. One literary element that a story needs is a character, which can either be a person or an animal.

▶ Use page 117 of *The Fox and the Crow* to answer the questions below.

1. What type of character is the Fox? Give examples from the text to support your answer.

_____

_____

_____

_____

2. How might this experience change the Crow? Why do you think so?

_____

_____

_____

▶ Use page 118 of *Raven and Crayfish* to answer the questions below.

3. Who is the trickster? Explain.

_____

_____

_____

_____

4. What does this tell you about Raven?

_____

_____

Word Sort: VCV Pattern

▶ Are the words sorted correctly? Draw a line through the words that are in the wrong column. Write them in the correct column.

Short Vowel Sound	Long Vowel Sound
habit	polite
relay	events
planet	unite
rapid	punish
relief	detail
motel	frozen

▶ Use the words from the chart to fill in the blanks. Write the correct word on the line. Do the words have a short vowel sound or a long vowel sound? Circle the ones that have a short vowel sound.

1. Something you do over and over again becomes a _____ .

2. The goal of the meeting was to _____ people with different points of view.

3. The word _____ can mean a type of race or to pass messages along.

4. When something is _____ it happens very quickly.

Name _____

Critical Vocabulary

You can use the words you learn from reading as you talk and write.

▷ **Use your understanding of the Critical Vocabulary words from *Ten Suns* to support your answers to the questions below. Then use the Critical Vocabulary words as you talk with a partner about your answers.**

1. When have you shown **gratitude** to someone?

_____

2. If you saw flowers that had **withered**, would you give them to a friend? Why or why not?

_____

3. What would you feel if you touched something that was **scorching**?

_____

4. What would you consider **reckless** behavior?

_____

5. Think of a time you **assumed** something. What could you have done instead?

_____

_____

6. How do you think it would feel to **prosper**?

_____

▷ **Write a sentence using two of the Critical Vocabulary words.**

_____

_____

Text and Graphic Features

> Use the print and video versions of *Ten Suns*, pages 134–135, to answer the questions below.

1. How does the illustration fit the description of Hu Yi?

_____

_____

_____

_____

2. How is this character portrayed in the video *The Ten Suns*?

_____

3. What description does the narrator give of Yi in the video?

_____

_____

> Review the end of *Ten Suns* and think about the video.

4. How does the video compare to the print version of this tale? What is the same? What is different?

_____

_____

_____

5. What connections can you make between the text and *The Ten Suns* video?

_____

Suffixes –ity and –ty

> Complete the chart with words that contain the suffix –*ity* or –*ty*.

–ity	–ty

> Write a sentence for each word in the chart.

_____

_____

_____

_____

_____

_____

_____

_____

_____

_____

Name _____

Media Techniques

The methods used to tell a story in video form are called **media techniques**.
Producers choose and combine different techniques to create the effects that best
tell the story.

Technique	What It Is
sound	voices, music, and other sound effects
voiceover	the voice of an unseen narrator who tells the story
visuals	all the types of images that viewers see
animation	a series of drawings or models that appear to move

When you watch a video, think about the choices the producer has made and how
these choices help viewers experience and understand important ideas.

> **Use the video and print versions, pages 138–140, of *Ten Suns* to answer the
> questions below.**

1. How are the illustrations in the video different from those in the text?

   _____

   _____

2. How do the sound effects and visuals in the video add to this tale?

   _____

   _____

3. How does the animation in the video help you understand this legend?

   _____

   _____

   _____

© Houghton Mifflin Harcourt Publishing Company. All rights reserved.

161

Module 7 • Week 3

Words with VCV Syllable Division Pattern

> **Read each sentence. Underline the word with the VCV pattern.**

1. The tornado siren is tested once a month.

2. We left our classroom the moment school was over.

3. We live on the planet Earth.

4. Our music festival occurs in April.

5. On field day we have many relay races.

6. It was a big relief when the test was over.

7. I have a habit of talking to myself.

8. Raoul has a great sense of humor.

9. Every detail of the book fair was organized.

10. We stayed at a nice motel on our trip.

Literary Elements

Literary elements include the characters, setting, plot, and events in a story.

> Use *Ten Suns*, pages 129–132, to answer the questions below.

1. Why do the boys decide to change their routine of walking across the sky?

_____

_____

2. Why do the boys get up early?

_____

_____

3. What problems do the boys' actions cause?

_____

_____

4. What is the cause of the ten suns in the sky?

_____

_____

> **Think about the sequence of events in the legend.**

5. With a partner, retell the events in sequence. Which events surprised you?

_____

_____

_____

_____

Name _____

VCCV and VCV Syllable Division Patterns

> Read each sentence. If the underlined word has a VCCV syllable pattern, write the word in the first column. If it has a VCV syllable pattern, write it in the second column.

VCCV	VCV

1. We will go shopping <u>after</u> we eat breakfast.

2. Our new <u>baby</u> is three weeks old.

3. Only one blueberry <u>muffin</u> was left on the tray.

4. The puppies are playing in the <u>basket</u>.

5. Our family had a <u>picnic</u> in the park.

6. Ten is an <u>even</u> number.

7. The <u>lady</u> wore a pretty red dress.

8. The beautiful <u>hotel</u> was very old.

Critical Vocabulary

You can use the words you learn from reading as you talk and write.

▶ **Use your understanding of the Critical Vocabulary words to help you finish each sentence.**

1. A flashlight is **convenient** to have when _____ .

2. Tonight's homework is time-**intensive** because _____ .

3. It was hard to stay **hydrated** yesterday because _____ .

4. We **transported** baked goods to the picnic in _____

_____ .

5. We used **disposable** plates and cups because _____

_____ .

6. One way to **assess** what you need for a trip is _____

_____ .

7. The article had a big **impact** because _____

_____ .

▶ **Choose two of the Critical Vocabulary words and use them in a sentence.**

_____

_____

Name _____

Author's Purpose

An **author's purpose** is his or her reason for writing. Knowing the author's purpose helps you determine what the author wants to do. To determine the author's purpose, ask, "Is the author writing to inform, entertain, or persuade?"

> **Reread the second box on page 158 in *Eco-Friendly Food*. Then answer the questions.**

1. Who do you think the author's intended audience is?

_____

_____

2. What does the author want readers to do? Use evidence for support.

_____

_____

_____

> **Reread page 164. Then answer the questions below.**

3. What is the purpose of the text on page 164?

_____

_____

4. What do you think the author wants readers to do after they read this selection?

_____

_____

VCCV and VCV Syllable Division Patterns

> Circle all words in the row having the same first vowel sound as the boldfaced word.

1. **basket**   magnet   appoint   napkin   master

2. **publish**   rubber   supper   bundle   super

3. **fifteen**   lilac   minor   kitten   pillow

4. **yellow**   message   began   female   rescue

5. **okay**   local   open   solid   solo

6. **bacon**   attic   navy   banner   table

7. **eagle**   before   gentle   even   errand

8. **silent**   window   item   title   tiger

9. **costume**   bottom   locate   clover   cotton

10. **music**   unicorn   number   public   unite

Latin Roots port, dict

The word *transported* contains the root *port* meaning "to carry."
The word *predict* contains the root *dict* meaning "to speak."

▸ **Complete the chart with other words that contain the roots *port* and *dict*.**

port	dict

▸ **Write a sentence for 4 words in the chart.**

_____

_____

_____

_____

_____

_____

_____

Ideas and Support

When authors present **ideas** and claims, they **support** them with facts, reasons, and other evidence. Evaluate the way an author supports an idea or claim by determining which statements are facts and which are opinions. Do this by reading each statement and asking, "Can this be proven to be true?"

> Read the list of pros and cons on page 160 of *Eco-Friendly Foods*. Then answer the questions below.

1. What is the claim about these foods?

   _____

2. What evidence does the author use to support this claim?

   _____

   _____

3. What evidence does the author use to argue against this claim?

   _____

> Reread paragraph 10 on page 162. Then answer the questions below.

4. What does the author want readers to understand about growing food?

   _____

   _____

5. What is one reason the author gives to support this claim?

   _____

   _____

Name _____

Text and Graphic Features

Authors of informational text often use **text and graphic features** to help organize the information, highlight key ideas, and support readers' understanding of the text. They use boldfaced words, headings, photographs, diagrams, charts, and graphs to help readers better understand the key ideas in a text.

> **Answer the questions about the first paragraph and the sidebar on page 161 of** *Eco-Friendly Food*.

1. What is the author's claim about bottled drinks?

_____

_____

2. How does the information in the sidebar support the author's claim?

_____

_____

_____

> **Look at the diagrams on page 163 to answer the questions below.**

3. Why is the text on page 163 numbered?

_____

_____

4. What do the diagrams show?

_____

5. Why do you think the author includes these visuals?

_____

6. How do these diagrams support your understanding of a cylinder garden?

_____

Words with the VCCV Syllable Division Pattern

> Complete each sentence with the best word from the word box. Then divide the word into syllables.

declare	whether	secret	apron	poster
degree	achieve	whiskers	chicken	bushel
ticket	author	rocket	gather	rather

1. Carla asked _____ the muffins were ready to eat.

2. The cat's _____ tickle my arm.

3. I suggest you wear this _____ before you start cooking.

4. Homemade _____ soup was cooking on the stove.

5. Gov. Smith will _____ the flooded land a disaster area.

6. We picked a _____ of apples from that tree.

7. A good writer will _____ information about a subject before writing.

8. The _____ has been on our classroom wall all year.

9. When my brother graduates from college he will earn a _____ .

10. O. Henry was a famous _____ of short stories.

Name _____

Critical Vocabulary

You can use the words you learn from reading as you talk and write.

> **Use your understanding of the Critical Vocabulary words to complete a word web for each word. Write words and phrases in the outer ovals that are related to the word in the center. Discuss your word webs with a partner.**

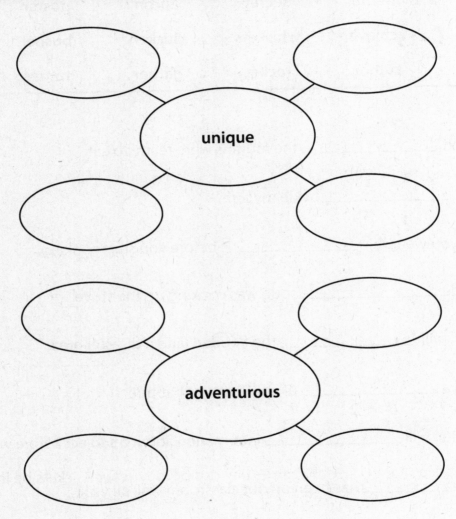

> **Use each of the Critical Vocabulary words in a sentence.**

_____

_____

Media Techniques

Media techniques include visual elements, such as action scenes, close-up views, and text boxes. Sound elements include narration. The narration is an important element in an informational video. The narrator needs to be an expert or someone who knows the topic well so that the viewer receives the correct information.

▶ **Review the visual elements in *Kids Rock Nutrition in the Kitchen*. Then answer the questions below.**

1. Identify the adult cook in the video. Is this person an expert in food preparation? How do you know?

   _____

   _____

   _____

2. Why do you think the video includes close-up views of a variety of vegetables?

   _____

   _____

   _____

▶ **Review the narration beginning at about 1:50 minutes into the video. Then answer the question below.**

3. If chicken takes longer to bake than fish, why can both types of packets be in the oven together at the same time?

   _____

   _____

   _____

Name _____

Words with the VCCV Syllable Division Pattern

▶ Draw a line between the syllables in the following VCCV words. Then write the words in the correct column.

puffin	declare	pocket	degree	rather
secret	clothing	tether	agree	monkey
gathering	rescuing	winter	poster	publishing
achievable	confide	subject	whether	apron

V / CCV	VCC / V	VC / CV

Prefixes sub-, fore-

> Complete the chart with words that contain the prefixes *sub*– and *fore*–.

sub–	fore–

> Write a sentence for four words in the chart.

_____

_____

_____

_____

_____

_____

_____

Name _____

Ideas and Support

In an argumentative text, an author states a **claim**. The author provides facts or examples to prove the claim is true. Sometimes an author includes an **opinion**. The opinion tells what the author thinks or feels about a subject, but the opinion cannot be proved true. No facts or examples are included to back up the opinion.

▶ **Reread paragraphs 5 and 6 on page 177 in *Bug Bites* to answer the questions.**

1. What claim does the author make?

_____

2. What facts or examples does the author provide to support this claim?

_____

_____

_____

▶ **Reread page 180 to answer the questions.**

3. How does the author support his opinion?

_____

_____

_____

4. What readers do you think the author had in mind when writing this text? Why do you think so?

_____

_____

_____

Words with the VCCCV Syllable Division Pattern

> Circle the consonant blend or digraph in each VCCCV word. Then divide the words into syllables and write the words in the correct column.

mischief	hundred	purchase	harmless
kingdom	athlete	although	explain
complete	middle	monster	supply

VC / CCV	VCC / CV

Critical Vocabulary

You can use the words you learn from reading as you talk and write.

> **Use your understanding of the Critical Vocabulary words to support your answers to the questions below. Then talk with a partner about your answers, using the Critical Vocabulary words.**

1. What kind of **culinary** skills do you have?

_____

2. What would you be **astounded** to see at school?

_____

3. Why might you be **crestfallen** after a game?

_____

4. What recipe would you **opt** to make for a cook-off?

_____

5. Why might a friend take **offense** at what you did?

_____

6. What do you think is **luscious**?

_____

7. How would you **react** if a pet snake got out of its cage?

_____

> **Write a sentence below using two Critical Vocabulary words.**

_____

_____

Name _____

Text and Graphic Features

Text features can present important parts of a story. Different kinds of type and punctuation may be used by an author to communicate something important or to get the reader's attention.

Graphic features are visuals, such as illustrations, diagrams, maps, and speech bubbles that help explain ideas in a text. In stories, graphic features may provide more details that were not provided to the reader in the story itself.

> ▶ **Answer the questions about page 192 of _Now You're Cooking!_**

1. What facial expression does each character have?

_____

2. Reread paragraphs 24–27. How do the illustrations add to your understanding of the story?

_____

_____

_____

> ▶ **Answer the questions about page 194 of _Now You're Cooking!_**

3. Read the ingredients for the recipe. What type of food does this recipe make?

_____

4. How do the illustrations on the page help you understand the recipe?

_____

Name _____

Greek Roots meter, therm, phon, tele

> Complete the chart with words that use the Greek roots *therm* and *tele*.
Underline or circle other Greek roots that combine with these to form new words.

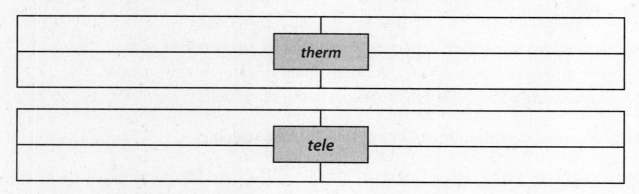

> Write a definition and sentence for 4 words in the chart.

_____

_____

_____

_____

_____

_____

_____

Idioms

An **idiom** is a phrase that means something different from what the individual words say. Idioms can make a story or text more interesting to read.

Examples: *a dime a dozen; a bee in your bonnet; beat around the bush*

> **Answer the question about page 187 of *Now You're Cooking!***

1. Reread paragraph 2. What does Avani mean when she uses the idiom "Now you're cooking"?

_____

_____

> **Answer the questions about paragraph 4 on page 188 of the story.**

2. What does the idiom "my goose is cooked" mean?

_____

3. What clues in the text help you understand the idiom?

_____

_____

> **Answer the questions about paragraphs 16–17 on page 190 of the story.**

4. What does the idiom "cook circles around you" mean?

_____

5. What does this idiom demonstrate in regards to how Martina is feeling about competing?

_____

Words with VCCCV Syllable Division Pattern

> Underline the consonant blend or consonant digraph in the VCCCV pattern. Then write the word dividing it into syllables.

1. pilgrim   _____   _____

2. sandwich   _____   _____

3. orchard   _____   _____

4. surprise   _____   _____

5. turtle   _____   _____

6. single   _____   _____

7. farther   _____   _____

8. sample   _____   _____

> **Choose four of the words and use them in sentences.**

_____

_____

_____

_____

Point of View

When you read a story, you need to know who the narrator, or storyteller, is. It's important to know from whose **point of view** the events are told. That's because different people can tell the same story different ways!

Stories are often told from a first-person or a third-person point of view.

First-Person Point of View The narrator . . .	Third-Person Point of View The narrator . . .
is a character in the story.	is someone outside the story.
tells his or her own thoughts and feelings.	tells the thoughts and feelings of others.
uses pronouns such as *I*, *me*, *my*, *mine*, and *we*.	uses pronouns such as *he*, *she*, *him*, *her*, *his*, *hers*, *they*, *them*, and *their*.

> **Answer the questions about page 187 of *Now You're Cooking!***

1. Reread paragraph 1. From which point of view is paragraph 1 being told?

_____

_____

2. Why does an author write a story in the third person?

_____

_____

> **Answer the question about page 193 of *Now You're Cooking!***

3. How do the characters add to the plot of the story?

_____

_____

Words with VV Syllable Division Pattern

> Read each sentence. Underline the word with the VV syllable division pattern in each sentence.

1. I'm afraid the rain will ruin your new hat.

2. The babies will sleep more easily in a quiet room.

3. "There will be a meteor shower next week," the news anchor stated.

4. The bear roamed the camping area looking for food.

5. The teachers will announce the winner of the poetry contest tomorrow.

> Underline the correct way to divide each boldfaced word into syllables.

1. dial	dia l	di al	d ial
2. violet	vi o let	vi olet	vio let
3. meow	me ow	me o w	meo w
4. science	sci en ce	scien ce	sci ence
5. diary	dia ry	di a ry	di ary

Critical Vocabulary

You can use the words you learn from reading as you talk and write.

> **Use your understanding of the Critical Vocabulary words to support your answers to the questions below.**

1. One meaning of the word **oasis** is a pool of water in the desert. How is this meaning like a park in a dirty city?

_____

_____

2. For what kind of project would you need **permission** from the school principal?

_____

_____

3. Why might someone be **installing** things in an **abandoned** house?

_____

_____

4. If you could choose a **frequent** activity, what would you choose and why?

_____

_____

5. How much daily exercise do you think is **sufficient** for someone your age?

_____

_____

> **Choose two of the Critical Vocabulary words and use them in a sentence. Include a synonym or antonym for one of the words.**

_____

_____

Name _____

Text and Graphic Features

In a graphic novel, text is used either as narration or as speech. Visuals such as diagrams and illustrations help explain ideas in the text.

> **Answer the questions about page 224 in *Luz Sees the Light*.**

1. Which text on the page is narration?

_____

_____

2. What purpose does this narration serve in the story?

_____

_____

3. What purpose do the drawings and speech balloons serve in this part of the story?

_____

_____

> **Answer the question about page 233 in *Luz Sees the Light*.**

4. What are three different ways in which text is used on this page?

_____

_____

Words with VV Syllable Division Pattern

> Read each sentence. Complete the sentence by choosing the word with the VV syllable division pattern. With this pattern both vowels are sounded.

1. Students can learn to skate by looking at this _____ .
   pamphlet   video

2. The child's toy was made of _____ plastic.
   pliable   flexible

3. Thelma is studying to be a _____ .
   dentist   librarian

4. The _____ was closed for remodeling.
   theater   hotel

5. Tyrone loves to read books on _____ .
   biology   chemistry

> Read the words in the box aloud. Circle all of the words in which you hear two different vowel sounds in the VV pattern.

refrain	teach	screen	dear	triumph
reality	break	diagram	could	trial
fluid	gradual	serial	explain	pail
pioneer	create	food	diet	client

Using Suffixes –*ible* and –*able*

The suffixes –*ible* and –*able* mean "able to" or "likely to" do or be something. They are used frequently in English words, usually after verbs, such as *believable* and *collapsible*.

> Complete the chart with other words that contain the suffix –*ible* or –*able*.

–*ible*	–*able*

> Write a sentence for each word in the chart.

_____

_____

_____

_____

_____

_____

_____

_____

_____

_____

_____

_____

Name _____

Theme

Knowing the **theme** helps you understand the main message, lesson, or moral of the text.

> **Answer the questions about page 216 in *Luz Sees the Light*.**

1. How does Luz want to change the empty lot?

_____

_____

2. What can you infer about the theme of the story from Luz's statement?

_____

_____

> **Answer the questions about page 238 in *Luz Sees the Light*.**

3. What story theme can you infer from Luz's words?

_____

_____

4. How does knowing the theme help you understand the story's events better?

_____

_____

Name _____

Idioms

An **idiom** is a type of common expression. An idiom means something different from the meaning of its individual words.

Knowing how to identify idioms helps you understand what the author has written.

> **Answer the questions about the idiom on page 223 in *Luz Sees the Light*.**

1. What does the idiom "out to lunch" mean?

_____

_____

2. What clues in the text help you understand the idiom?

_____

_____

> **Answer the questions about the idiom in the middle row on page 228 in *Luz Sees the Light*.**

3. What does the idiom "on board" mean?

_____

_____

4. What clues in the text help you understand the idiom?

_____

_____

Final Schwa + /r/ Sound

beggar	finger	birdwatcher	cedar	traitor	sugar
doctor	partner	visitor	enter	actor	fever
teacher	author	polar	harbor	cellar	banner

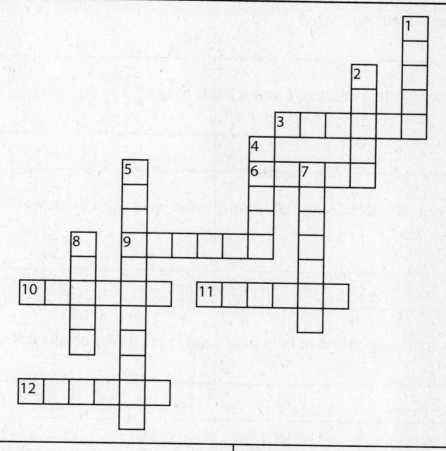

Across

3. any one of five digits on a hand

6. to go into a place

9. medical person who treats patients

10. an underground room

11. place where ships dock

12. a flag

Down

1. a high rise in body temperature

2. food item used to sweeten something

4. an evergreen tree

5. person who observes birds

7. person who betrays his country

8. having to do with the North or South Pole

Name _____

Critical Vocabulary

You can use the words you learn from reading as you talk and write.

> **Use your understanding of the Critical Vocabulary words to support your answers to the questions below.**

1. What are you **obsessed** with? Why?

_____

2. Why do teachers give little children **blunt** scissors to use?

_____

_____

3. If you passed a door marked "Army **Recruiting**," what would you think they probably do there?

_____

_____

4. Would you like to be **appointed** to help plan a class party? Why or why not?

_____

_____

5. What might cause a sea creature to become **stranded** and **disoriented** on the shore?

_____

_____

> **Choose two of the Critical Vocabulary words and use them in a sentence. Include either a synonym or an antonym of the vocabulary word in the sentence.**

_____

_____

Name _____

Figurative Language

When authors use **figurative language**, they use words and phrases that have meanings beyond the strict dictionary definitions. Authors use figurative language:

• to make their writing interesting.
• to help readers create an image or picture in their minds.

	What It Is	Examples
Sensory Language	Words that tell how something looks, sounds, feels, tastes, or smells	*A turtle's stubby tail* *Scorching hot sand*
Simile	Comparing two things using the word *like* or *as*	*The scared boy stood* like *a statue.* *This shell is as smooth as glass.*
Metaphor	Comparing two things without using *like* or *as*	*Our city streets are a maze.* *The turtle's flipper is a steam shovel.*
Sound Device	A sound pattern used to draw readers' attention to or emphasize certain lines in a piece of writing	*Two tiny turtles*

> **Answer the questions about page 251 in** *On Sea Turtle Patrol.*

1. What simile describes how Callie feels as she runs?

_____

2. What does the simile mean?

_____

3. Which sensory details describe what the first boy on the bike looks like?

_____

> **Answer the question about paragraph 52 on page 253 in** *On Sea Turtle Patrol.*

4. What examples of alliteration are in this paragraph?

_____

Final Syllable (r-controlled vowel)
Final Schwa + /r/ Sound

> **Add er, ar, or or to each base word.**

contract	pill	command
beg	publish	direct
develop	sail	cell

> **Then sort the words by the spelling of the final schwa + /r/ sound.**

–ar	–er	–or

Name _____

Critical Vocabulary

You can use the words you learn from reading as you talk and write.

> **Use your understanding of the Critical Vocabulary words to support your answers to the questions below. Then use the Critical Vocabulary words as you talk with a partner about your answers.**

1. When and why is it important to **estimate**?

_____

_____

_____

2. If someone said, "I wish things wouldn't **decay**," what would you tell them?

_____

_____

_____

> **Use the two Critical Vocabulary words in a sentence. Include either a synonym or an antonym of the vocabulary word in the sentence.**

_____

_____

_____

_____

_____

_____

Name 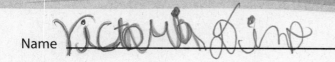 Victoria Slino

Text and Graphic Features

In nonfiction texts, authors often draw attention to key ideas with **text and graphic features**.

Feature	What It Is	Purpose
Headings	Type that is larger than other text; may be a different color	To show the topic of a section of text
Captions	Text that appears near a photograph or other image	To explain more about an image
Graphs	Images that show connections between amounts	To show amounts in a visual way; to show how an amount relates to a total

> **Answer the questions about pages 260–263 of** *How Can We Reduce Household Waste?*

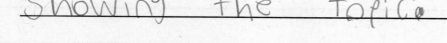
420-423

1. How does the author use headings to organize the story?

    Showing the topic.

2. How does the circle graph on page 260 connect to the text?

    _____

> **Answer the question about the caption on page 261.**

3. What information does the caption add to what is shown in the photograph?

    _____

> **Answer the question about the graph on page 274.**

4. How does the graph add to your understanding of the text on page 274?

    _____

Using Suffixes –ful, –ous, –less

The suffix –*ful* means "full of." The suffix –*ous* means "having" or "possessing." The suffix –*less* means "without."

▶ **Complete the chart with words that contain the suffix –*ful*, –*ous*, or –*less*.**

–*ful*	–*ous*	–*less*

▶ **Write a sentence for six of the words in the chart.**

_____

_____

_____

_____

_____

_____

_____

_____

_____

_____

_____

Name _____

Ideas and Support

When authors write an argumentative text, they present a **claim**, or idea. They think about who their readers are because they want those readers to believe their claim or to take action. Authors **support**, or back up, their claim with reasons and other evidence that their readers will understand.

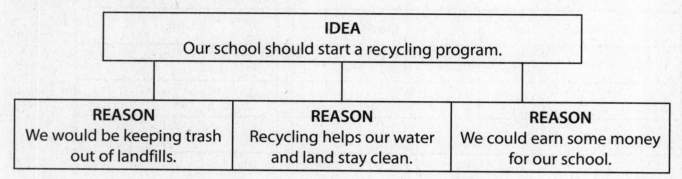

Authors provide evidence to show that their reasons make sense. A **fact** is a statement that is true and can be proved. Facts help readers understand why they should agree with a claim.

▶ **Answer the questions about paragraphs 24 and 25 of** *How Can We Reduce Household Waste?*

1. What claim does the author make?

_____

2. What facts or examples does the author provide to support this claim?

_____

_____

▶ **Think about the text** *How Can We Reduce Household Waste?*

3. What audience do you think the author had in mind when writing this text? Why do you think so?

_____

_____

Words with Final Stable Syllable
Final Schwa + /l/ Sound

1. Complete this story by writing in each blank the correct word with the indicated
final schwa + /l/ sound from the word box.

eagle	article	barrel	animal	gentle
metal	squirrel	special	marvel	coastal

My teacher asked me to write an _____ [-*le*] for our class newspaper.

I wasn't sure what to write about. Maybe I could write a story about an _____

[-*al*]. There are many different ones to choose from. I thought about our rabbit, which

is _____ [-*le*]. Then I thought about a _____ [-*el*] with its nest of acorns.

Should I research our nation's symbol, the _____ [-*le*]? Or would a _____ [-*al*]

bird like the pelican make my writing _____ [-*al*]?

2. Write two or more sentences telling which animal you think the author should
choose. Include three words with the final schwa + /l/ sound. Underline the letters
that make the final schwa sound in each word.

_____

_____

_____

_____

Name _____

Critical Vocabulary

You can use the words you learn from reading as you talk and write.

> **Use your understanding of the Critical Vocabulary words to support your answers to the questions below.**

1. If someone asked, "Who were your **ancestors**?" what would you say?

   _____

   _____

2. If you drew a picture of a **swirl**, what would it look like?

   _____

   _____

3. Would you swim in water that had fast **currents**? Why or why not?

   _____

   _____

4. Why might someone **sneer** at an **outspoken** person?

   _____

   _____

5. How do you **envision** a **canopy** of trees? How does it move?

   _____

   _____

> **Choose two of the Critical Vocabulary words and use them in a sentence.**

   _____

   _____

Name _____

Author's Craft

Author's craft is anything done by a writer to make the writing look or sound a certain way. **Voice** and **anecdotes** are both elements of author's craft. An anecdote is a short, funny, or interesting story about a person or an event.

> **Reread page 280 in *Seeds of Change* and then answer the questions below.**

1. Why does the author begin the biography with this anecdote?

_____

_____

2. How does the author use language to appeal to your senses and to describe actions in a vivid way?

_____

_____

_____

_____

> **Reread paragraph 10 in *Seeds of Change*. Answer the question.**

3. How does the author's use of similes help you understand Wangari's focus on her brother's teaching?

_____

_____

> **Answer the question about the anecdote on page 294.**

4. Why does the author include this anecdote?

_____

_____

Name _____

Using Suffixes –ic, –en

The suffix –ic means "of or relating to." The suffix –en means "to give or have the characteristics."

> Complete the chart with words that contain the suffix –ic or –en.

–ic	–en

> Write a sentence for each word in the chart.

_____

_____

_____

_____

_____

_____

_____

_____

_____

_____

_____

_____

Name _____

Literary Elements

Literary elements are the pieces that make up a story, such as characters, setting, plot, and events. Identifying and analyzing these elements can help you better understand a biography.

> **Revisit pages 280–285 in *Seeds of Change*. Then answer the questions.**

1. Who is this biography mainly about?

_____

_____

2. Who are some secondary characters?

_____

_____

> **Answer the questions about pages 288 and 289 in *Seeds of Change*.**

3. What is the setting in this illustration?

_____

_____

4. What details from the text support your thinking?

_____

_____

_____

_____

Name _____

Words with Final Schwa + /l/ Sound

> Choose the word with the schwa + /l/ sound to complete the sentence. Write it in the blank and underline the letters that stand for the final schwa + /l/ sound.

1. The _____ was filled with rainwater.
       bucket   barrel

2. The _____ clown juggled six balls at once.
       carnival   circus

3. The prince lived in a _____ surrounded by a moat.
       castle   mansion

4. The _____ vase broke when it hit the floor.
       glass   crystal

5. The snowflakes _____ as they float down from the sky.
       sparkle   glisten

6. My _____ is very obedient and always sits when I tell her to.
       poodle   puppy

7. Jane has a tea _____ that whistles when water boils.
       pitcher   kettle

8. A kitten is a _____ pet for children.
       gentle   lovely

Name _____

Text Structure

Authors organize texts in many different ways. The **text structure** they use depends on what they are writing. Paying attention to text structure can help a reader better understand and follow along with information in a text. Writers of biographies often use chronological order to describe the events in a person's life in the order in which they occurred.

> **Reread page 284 in *Seeds of Change*. Then answer the question.**

1. What happens after Wangari starts school?

_____

_____

_____

> **Answer the questions about page 288 of *Seeds of Change*.**

2. What important events occur in Wangari's life after she starts school in the city? List them in sequential order.

_____

_____

_____

_____

3. Why does the author include all these events?

_____

_____

_____

Multisyllabic Words

> Read each sentence. Choose the three-syllable word that correctly completes the sentence. Write the word on the line. Then divide the word into syllables.

1. My sister loves that movie because it is the _____ .
scariest   nicest   cutest

2. Sasha likes to play the _____ in the school band.
trumpet   flute   clarinet

3. There is a famous _____ on the island.
mountain   plateau   volcano

4. Joe's favorite food is _____ and meatballs.
spaghetti   pepperoni   noodles

5. Junko's favorite school subject is _____ .
mathematics   history   geometry

6. Inez's father traveled to Spain for _____ .
vacation   business   health

7. It's raining, so Mom told me to take my _____ .
umbrella   poncho   raincoat

8. Smile, so the _____ can take your picture.
artist   camera   photographer

9. When is Carla going to the _____ ?
movies   celebration   festival

Name _____

Critical Vocabulary

You can use the words you learn from reading as you talk and write.

▶ **Use your understanding of the Critical Vocabulary words to support your answers to the questions below. Then use the Critical Vocabulary words as you talk with a partner about your answers.**

1. What single item would **significantly** improve your life?

   _____

   _____

2. What person has **enabled** you to do something you would not have done on your own?

   _____

   _____

3. If you could own the **patent** for something, what would it be?

   _____

   _____

4. What would be a **peak** experience for you?

   _____

   _____

5. What message would you want **transmitted** to your best friend?

   _____

   _____

6. What flowers should *not* be **plucked**?

_____

_____

7. If you **proposed** a movie to watch tonight, what movie would it be?

_____

_____

8. If you wanted to run for class president, how would you **influence** others to vote for you?

_____

_____

▶ **Write sentences below using two Critical Vocabulary words.**

_____

_____

Text Structure

Text structure refers to how the information in a text is organized. Authors use a comparison/contrast structure to describe how things are alike and different, a cause/effect structure to show what happened and why, a sequence structure to explain events in order, and a problem/solution structure to show a problem and how it is solved.

▶ **Answer the questions about pages 318–319 of *The History of Communication*.**

1. What is the text structure of paragraphs 22–25? How do you know?

_____

_____

2. How does knowing the text structure help you understand the main idea in paragraphs 22–25?

_____

_____

▶ **Choose another section of text in *The History of Communication*.**

3. What is the text structure?

_____

_____

4. How does knowing the text structure help you understand the main idea in this section?

_____

_____

Name _____

Multisyllabic Words

▶ Choose the correct syllabication for each word. Underline the stressed syllable.

1. po ta to   pot at o   po tat o

2. glo ri ous   glor i ous   glori ous

3. im port ant   imp or tant   im por tant

4. re new al   renew al   re ne wal

5. exam ple   ex amp le   ex am ple

6. vert i cal   ver ti cal   ver tic al

7. mus i cal   mu si cal   mu sic al

8. exc ell ent   excel lent   ex cel lent

Name _____

Latin Roots tele, port, graph

The roots *tele*, *port*, and *graph* have Latin origins.
The meaning of the root *tele* is "at a distance."
The meaning of the root *port* is "to carry."
The meaning of the root *graph* is "to write."

> Complete the chart with words that contain the roots *tele*, *port*, and *graph*.

tele	port	graph

> Write a sentence each for three of the words in the chart.

_____

_____

_____

_____

_____

_____

_____

_____

Name _____

Central Idea

The **central idea** in a text is the most important idea the author wants the reader to think about. The author supports the central, or main, idea with details.

▶ **Answer the questions about pages 314–315 in *The History of Communication*.**

1. What is the central, or main, idea of the section "The Telegraph"?

_____

_____

2. What details in the text support the central, or main, idea?

_____

_____

_____

▶ **Answer the questions about page 324 in *The History of Communication*.**

3. What is the central, or main, idea of the section "The Internet"?

_____

_____

4. What details does the author use to support the central, or main, idea on this page?

_____

_____

_____

Name _____

Text and Graphic Features

Informational text often includes **text features** such as headings and boldfaced words. Informational text usually includes one or more **graphic features** such as photographs, diagrams, and illustrations.

> **Revisit page 317 in *The History of Communication*. Then answer the questions.**

1. What unique text or graphic feature do you notice on page 317? What information does it give?

   _____

   _____

> **Reread paragraph 25 in *The History of Communication*. Then answer the question.**

2. How do the photograph and caption on page 319 connect to the text in paragraph 25? How do the photograph and caption add to your understanding of the ideas in the text?

   _____

   _____

> **Revisit pages 320–321 and answer the questions.**

3. How does the diagram on page 320 connect to the text in paragraph 30?

   _____

   _____

4. How does the diagram add to your understanding of the ideas in the text?

   _____

   _____

Words with Silent Consonants

> Complete the crossword puzzle using words from the word box.
Circle the silent consonant in each word.

handsome
comb
wreath
half
limb
kneel
tomb
gnarled
wrestled
fetch
listen
history
yolk
calm
folktale
plumber
honest
doubt

Across

  4. pay attention to a speaker

  5. quiet and peaceful

  8. to be uncertain about something

  9. someone who always tells the truth

11. a branch of the tree

Down

  1. flowers and greenery arranged in a circle

  2. the yellow part of an egg

  3. twisted and tangled; not straight

  5. make hair smooth and neat

  6. to go get something

  7. a story passed down through the years

10. a burial place

Name _____

Critical Vocabulary

You can use the words you learn from reading as you talk and write.

▶ **Use your understanding of the Critical Vocabulary words to support your answers to the questions below. Then use the Critical Vocabulary words as you talk with a partner about your answers.**

1. What kind of new technology might cause widespread **astonishment**? Explain.

_____

_____

2. Do you think **gestures** are an important part of public speaking? Why or why not?

_____

_____

3. What do **linguists** study?

_____

_____

4. Humans have an **instinct** to communicate. What **instincts** do animals have?

_____

_____

▶ **Write a sentence below using two Critical Vocabulary words.**

_____

_____

Name _____

Text Structure

The way an author organizes and connects ideas in a text is called **text structure**. Identifying text structure helps readers understand an author's main ideas. Authors might organize their ideas in one or more of these ways:

Text Structure	What It Does
Cause/Effect	Explains what happened and why
Problem/Solution	Describes a problem and its solution
Chronological	Tells events in the order they happened

▶ **Reread paragraphs 4 and 5 in *A New Language—Invented by Kids!* Then answer the questions.**

1. What text structure does the author use in this part of the text?

_____

_____

2. How does knowing the text's structure help you understand the main idea of these paragraphs?

_____

_____

▶ **Reread page 333 in *A New Language—Invented by Kids!* and answer the question.**

3. How does the author use chronological events to support the main idea?

_____

_____

_____

Name _____

Words with Silent Consonants

▶ Choose the correct word from the word box to complete each sentence. Underline the silent consonant in the word.

climb	wreath	gnarled	listen	knuckle
handsome	hasten	wrinkle	comb	yolk
calm	tomb	answer	honest	fetch
folktale	limb	half	plumber	kneel

1. The girl wore a beautiful _____ of flowers in her hair.

2. Our teacher read us a _____ from Germany.

3. When the sink was stopped up, we called a _____ .

4. The _____ old tree in the town square was a hundred years old.

5. Our group must _____ if we want to make the meeting.

6. A _____ is a handy thing to carry in a pocket.

7. The twins taught their dog, Sparky, to _____ .

8. An _____ person is worthy of respect.

9. George could not figure out the _____ to my riddle.

10. A leopard is able to _____ a tree.

Critical Vocabulary

You can use the words you learn from reading as you talk and write.

> **Use your understanding of the Critical Vocabulary words to support your answers to the questions below. Then use the Critical Vocabulary words as you talk with a partner about your answers.**

1. How would you design a backpack so that it was both **practical** and stylish?

_____

_____

2. When might a simple task seem like a major **operation**?

_____

_____

3. How important is it for your clothing to be **immaculate**?

_____

_____

> **Write a sentence below using two Critical Vocabulary words.**

_____

_____

_____

_____

Name _____

Media Techniques

The methods used to tell a story in video form are called **media techniques**.
Producers choose and combine different techniques to create the effects that
best tell the story.

Technique	What It Is
Sound	Voices, music, and other sound effects
Voice-over	The voice of an unseen narrator who tells the story
Visuals	All the types of images that viewers see
Live action	Real people and animals who are part of the action
Animation	A series of drawings or models that appear to move

When you watch a video, think about the choices the producer has made and how
they help viewers experience and understand important ideas.

> **Answer the questions about the media techniques used in _Dolphin Dinner_.**

1. Which media techniques does this video use?

_____

2. How does the music support the events in the video? Explain.

_____

_____

_____

3. How do the media techniques support the video's purpose?

_____

_____

Name _____

Unusual Spelling Patterns

▶ **Choose a word in each row that has the same vowel sound as the bold letters in the first word.**

1. unpl**ea**sant   necktie   seaplane   eyelid

2. disg**ui**se   rebirth   realize   rebuild

3. unfortun**ate**   celebrate   flashlight   bandit

4. reb**ui**ld   unfilled   refined   retried

5. re**new**al   refused   disputed   unloosened

▶ **Use the first word in each row in an original sentence.**

_____

_____

_____

_____

_____

_____

_____

_____

Unusual Spelling Patterns

> Read each sentence. Write the word from the box that best replaces the underlined word or words in each sentence. Underline the unusual spelling pattern. Circle the sound that the unusual spelling pattern makes.

research	unbelievable	unguarded	submarine
unpleasant	subtitle	unfortunate	untypical
recycle	disguise	rebuild	refuel

Sentence	Word	Sound
1. Jack's story was so <u>outrageous</u> that we began to laugh.	_____	/ē/ /ō/
2. The city will <u>construct again</u> the monument destroyed by the tornado.	_____	/ĭ/ /ŭ/
3. The diner's food was so <u>yucky</u>, we could not eat it.	_____	/ē/ /ĕ/
4. That behavior is <u>not usual</u> of that kind of animal.	_____	/ĭ/ /ī/
5. Wade was <u>unrecognizable</u> in his costume.	_____	/ĭ/ /ī/
6. The students had to <u>look up</u> information on the topic.	_____	/ər/ /är/
7. The <u>vehicle</u> can travel underwater.	_____	/ă/ /ē/
8. The castle was left <u>without protection</u>.	_____	/ur/ /är/
9. It was <u>unlucky</u> that I missed my plane.	_____	/ĭ/ /ē/
10. Many communities try to <u>reuse</u> certain materials, including paper, glass, plastic, and metal.	_____	/ĭ/ /ī/

Name _____

Author's Craft

Author's craft is the language and techniques authors use to make their stories more interesting. Author's craft techniques also communicate ideas to the reader.

> **Reread paragraphs 20–22 in *Cooper's Lesson* and then answer the questions.**

1. What does "Cooper's heart sank" mean? What does "his tongue lay as heavy and still in his mouth as a dead fish" mean?

   _____

   _____

2. How do these phrases contribute to the author's voice?

   _____

   _____

> **Reread paragraphs 60–64 in *Cooper's Lesson*. Then answer the questions.**

3. Why does the author use this anecdote?

   _____

   _____

4. How does the anecdote help readers better understand the characters?

   _____

   _____

Name _____

Homophones: Using Context to Determine Meaning

▶ Choose the correct word to complete each sentence. Write it on the line. Underline the context clue that helped you choose the correct word.

1. When Grandpa went on a trip, he promised to _____ postcards to us.
   right   write

2. I was so hungry that I _____ four pieces of pizza.
   eight   ate

3. When Katrina was sick, she was _____ from her fever.
   week   weak

4. The _____ wore armor to protect himself and his horse.
   knight   night

5. When we were making the cake, we ran out of _____ .
   flower   flour

6. Juan finished the _____ puzzle by himself.
   hole   whole

7. We had to _____ in line for an hour to buy the tickets.
   wait   weight

8. As Mom was driving, she stepped on the _____ to avoid hitting the squirrel.
   break   brake

9. The weary travelers stayed at a small _____ by the ocean.
   inn   in

10. When we went to camp, we _____ horses.
    road   rode

Name _____

Homophones

> Read each clue. Choose a homophone from the box that matches the context of each clue. Write the word in the puzzle.

chews	toe	rows	peace	hall
waste	piece	jeans	sale	heard
plane	choose	herd	tow	rose
allowed	haul	aloud	plain	sail

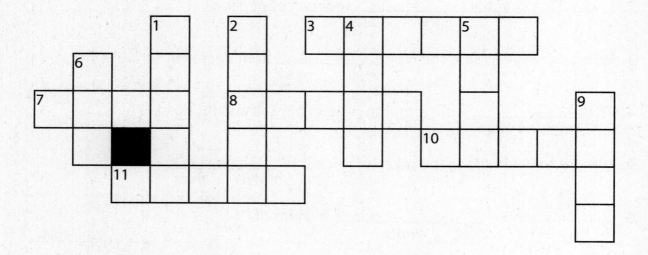

Across

3. to pick one thing instead of another

7. the way crops are planted in fields

8. to say something so others can hear

10. quiet

11. pants made of heavy cotton

Down

1. to throw away things without using them

2. a flat area of level land

4. to transport goods over distances

5. when stores discount their merchandise

6. one of the 10 digits on your feet

9. a group of cows

Name _____

Recognize Root Words

> Read each sentence. Underline the word containing a suffix. Write the root word in the first column and the suffix in the second column.

Sentence	Root Word	Suffix
1. Yesterday was cloudier than today.		
2. That character is the strangest one in the story.		
3. The street was quieter when it became dark.		
4. The youngest person in the family is two years old.		
5. The athlete's breathing was rapid after the race.		
6. The beach is smoother by the ocean.		
7. Mark solved the math problem correctly.		
8. That small knife is the sharpest one.		
9. Are you sure this measurement is accurate?		
10. This puzzle is the easiest one on the shelf.		

Recognize Root Words

▷ **Read each sentence. Circle the word that has a prefix or suffix. Then write the root word on the line.**

1. The storm made swimming dangerous.   _____

2. The strongman made weightlifting look effortless.   _____

3. We listened closely to the weather report.   _____

4. We were able to find a replacement for the part.   _____

5. We were uncertain about our science project.   _____

6. Liz had many colorful seashells.   _____

7. Adam gave the adorable dog a treat.   _____

8. She bought the fanciest dress.   _____

9. The street crew will remove the snow.   _____

10. Uncle Pete was uninjured in the accident.   _____

Multisyllabic Words with Affixes

▶ Read each sentence. Underline the word that has a prefix or suffix. Then write the word in the correct box, circling the affix.

1. This story is the craziest one I have ever read.

2. Would you untangle this knot for me?

3. The woman gave an incorrect answer on the quiz show.

4. I want to reimagine the event.

5. She accidentally dropped the book.

6. Sean played the piano superbly at the concert.

7. This chair is very uncomfortable.

8. The magician made the rabbit disappear.

Prefix	Suffix

Multisyllabic Words with Affixes

> Add one of the following prefixes to each base word to make its opposite.

| in– | dis– | un– | mis– |

easy		definite	
honest		forgivable	
dependent		behave	
fasten		represent	
identify		obey	

Choose the word with the correct affixes to fit the meaning.

reheated	rewind	underwater	preheat	misprint	previewed
disable	reviewed	replaying	unable	reprint	unwind

1. to heat before _____

2. to print wrongly _____

3. below the water _____

4. playing again _____

5. viewed before _____

6. to wind again _____

Name _____

Review Syllable Division Patterns

▶ Read each sentence and look at the clue at the end. Choose the word that makes the most sense in the blank, and write the word on the line. Then divide that word into syllables. You will only use a word one time, and there will be words not used.

V/V	V/CV	VC/V
dial	deny	cabin
fluids	ocean	talent
create	frozen	limit
lion	pilot	novel

1. Many amazing sea creatures live in the _____ . (V/CV)

2. My little brother was scared by the roar of the _____ . (V/V)

3. Last summer, we spent a week in a _____ in the mountains. (VC/V)

4. Could you please turn down the volume by using the _____? (V/V)

5. I really enjoyed reading the adventure _____ . (VC/V)

6. She has such musical _____! (VC/V)

7. It is important to drink a lot of _____ when you exercise. (V/V)

8. The _____ landed the airplane safely. (V/CV)

9. In art class, we were able to _____ a sculpture with clay. (V/V)

10. The children were ice skating on the _____ pond. (V/CV)

Name _____

Review Syllable Division Patterns

> Read each sentence. Look at the word choices beneath the sentence, and write the one that would make the most sense on the line. Then draw a line between the syllables in the word you chose.

1. My favorite food is cheese _____ .
   cherry   pizza   pumpkin

2. I needed to _____ the shirt for a bigger size.
   button   transfer   exchange

3. My dad used the _____ to smooth the surface of the wood.
   sandpaper   slipper   ostrich

4. We could hear the chirp of the _____ in the darkness.
   sandwich   cricket   children

5. Although the sweater was warm, it was very _____ .
   athletic   constant   itchy

6. Our puppy gets into a lot of _____ when left alone.
   mischief   concrete   zipper

7. The smell of baking cookies filled the _____ .
   district   kitchen   neighborhood

8. The _____ jumped high above the waves of the ocean.
   farmer   rabbit   dolphin

Name _____

Compound Words

> Read the sentences carefully. Circle the compound word you see in each sentence. After the sentence, write the words that make up the compound word you found.

1. I climbed the staircase to go to my room. _____, _____

2. The toothpaste had a refreshing mint flavor. _____, _____

3. The guard helped the students at the crosswalk. _____, _____

4. The moonlight reflected brightly off the pond. _____, _____

5. When it was time to leave, I waved goodbye. _____, _____

6. Deanna likes to catch fireflies in the summer. _____, _____

7. The teacher wrote the problem on the blackboard. _____, _____

8. My brother's favorite sport is football. _____, _____

9. I felt homesick when I went to camp last summer. _____, _____

10. Could you put this magazine on the bookshelf? _____, _____

Name _____

Multisyllabic Compound Words

▶ **Read each sentence and the words in the box below. Find a word from the box that makes sense in the sentence, and write it on the line. Write the smaller words that make up the compound word on the lines after the sentence. Then divide these words into syllables.**

underwater	grandmother
fingernails	overdue
sandpaper	fisherman
strawberry	housekeeper
saltwater	screwdriver

1. I spread the gooey _____ jam on my toast. _____, _____

2. Mariah painted her _____ a bright pink color. _____, _____

3. Dad used the _____ to put the new bike together. _____, _____

4. We went to the library to return the _____ books. _____, _____

5. Many tropical fish live in _____. _____, _____

6. The _____ packed his pole, net, bait, and bucket into the boat. _____, _____

7. I look forward to visiting my _____ because she is a great cook. _____, _____

8. Jamal used the _____ to smooth the wood of his bookshelf. _____, _____

Name _____

Multisyllabic Words

▶ Read each sentence. Circle the multisyllabic word that has a prefix, suffix, or inflectional ending added to a root word. Divide the word into syllables. Then write the root word on the line provided.

1. My dad is fixing the old car. _____

2. Would you like to go bowling? _____

3. The governor rode in the parade. _____

4. We put all of the food in the refrigerator. _____

5. The child said, "Please go away!" _____

6. I quickly ate my lunch. _____

7. The shop had many cute dresses in the window. _____

8. I walk our dog around the block each day. _____

9. My mom used fresh pumpkins to make the pie. _____

10. We had to walk briskly to get to school on time. _____

Name _____

Multisyllabic Words

▷ Read each sentence and look at the clue at the end. Choose the word that makes the most sense in the blank, and write the word on the line. Then divide that word into syllables. You will only use a word one time, and there will be words not used.

V/CV	VC/V	VC/CV
tiny	never	dinner
crocus	column	index
recite	talent	confess
cement	hazard	sandals

1. The workers poured _____ to make the sidewalk. (V/CV)

2. We ate chicken for _____ yesterday. (VC/CV)

3. What act will you perform for the _____ show? (VC/V)

4. Did you pack a pair of _____ for the beach? (VC/CV)

5. The new mother held her _____ baby. (V/CV)

6. I've _____ seen that TV show. (VC/V)

7. I looked in the _____ of the book. (VC/CV)

8. My mom planted the _____ bulbs in the garden. (V/CV)

9. My dad drove carefully around the _____ in the road. (VC/V)

10. Can you _____ the poem for the class? (V/CV)